THE UNVEILING OF JESUS

Volume 1

John Brusseau

A Book by John Brusseau

ISBN: 979-8-218-04266-0

INTRODUCTION

Our world is stuffed full of ideas about what a human is and what ails our species. Psychologists, religionists, philosophers, scientists, and a myriad of self-help authors have all weighed in at great length about the human condition. And with all of this input, almost no one has a clear grasp or significant insight into the most basic questions and problems facing us. Who out there has an overview, a big picture that can help us get a grasp of this human existence thing? No more esoteric mumblings, and no more academic verbal spasms of fifty-dollar words and ideas so disconnected from our experience of life that we choke on their useless abstractions. Surely someone has a grasp of these matters important to us all.

What if I told you that hidden within the bible, that ancient foundation of Judaic and Christian orthodoxy, that book we take to Sunday school, swear oaths to, and argue about incessantly, holds within its series of stories a perfect big picture of our species' psychological problems? And what if I told you that the last book, that miserably incomprehensible book of prophecy known as The Book of Revelation, perfectly sums up this big picture in a most profound way?

Do you want to know how genuine change for the better takes place?

Do you want to know how things went wrong for you, for us all?

Do you want a real solution to all of your human problems, and want it explained in terms you can easily understand, in concepts that resonate with your experience of life?

This book is written to show you that big picture that is the bible, and it homes in on the summation of that big picture, The Unveiling of Jesus. This book on the Unveiling of Jesus is not some mystical interpretation of biblical prophecy. It is a focus on the overall picture the bible means to give us, a picture that is most healing, most transformative.

May the God who is love bless your reading of this book.

TABLE OF CONTENTS

INTRODUCTION... iii

TABLE OF CONTENTS... v

THE STRUCTURE.. vii

THE PURPOSE OF THIS BOOK ix

CHAPTER 1 – JESUS JUDGES THE ECCLESIA............................... 1

Rev. 1:1-12 Introduction to Jesus' Judgment on the Ecclesia 1

Here Is A Biblical Summary Of The Underlying Psychological Equation Defining Our Species Many Psychological Issues....... 15

Fertility Cults and the Revelation of Jesus.. 17

Daniel's Prophecy 27

OVERVIEW OF THE UNVEILING OF JESUS 28

Our Destiny (our course) as Followers of Jesus 32

Revelation 1:12-20 What It's All About.. 37

And having turned I saw seven golden candlesticks; 38

Rev. 2-3 The Application 50

Catalyst -Ephesus Rev. 2:1-7 52

SYSTEM - Smyrna Pergamum, Thyatira Rev. 2:8-11 66

Smyrna 67

Pergamum Rev. 2:12-17 72

Thyatira Rev. 2:18-29 78

What idolatry was in Old Covenant times, self-righteous
    legalism is in ours 86

Outcome -Sardis, Laodicea, Philadelphia 90

Sardis Rev. 3:1-6 90

Philadelphia Rev. 3:7-13 95

Laodicea Rev. 3:14-22 101

Observe What Jesus Says To The Self-Righteous,
    Legalistic Hypocrites Of His Day. 103

ON IDOLATRY 118

THE STRUCTURE

You will see the presence of triads throughout this section. This triad is ubiquitous in the unfolding of the universe. It is how things unfold in the material universe, in three stages, or on three levels. The first stage is the intrinsic stage, in which the essence of something (its truth) is active. The second stage is the systematic embodiment of that intrinsic factor. This second stage is like a wife for the husband-like intrinsic stage. Just as a wife through union with the husband systematically generates life that is an expression of the two of them, so too does the system generate all that exists in the material universe. The third stage is thus the outcome stage of things. It is given birth to by the systemic stage.

Everything in the material universe is playing out in one of these three stages (CATALYST/SYSTEM/OUTCOME), and the role associated with it. This kind of structure is embedded in the Book of Revelation as well. To be aware of this fundamental structure of things is to more clearly grasp what is being expressed in this revelation. For example, in as much as the Unveiling of Jesus is also an unveiling of God's resolution/judgment of every problem in the universe, what we are shown is first, God giving us the divine, and perfect standard of how things are meant to be. Then we see God showing us what is wrong. And finally, we see what He is going to do to fix things.

I should also mention that my experience working with the dreams of people has shaped how I see the message given us in the Unveiling of Jesus. For example, I note that the structure and patterns I have seen in the Unveiling are remarkably similar to the structure one finds in dreams. And yes, these sequences follow a catalyst/system/outcome pattern. There are (and you could see this were you to remember your dreams fully) typically, multiple sequences in dreams. In each succeeding sequence, the dream is restarted and unfolds, covering the same issues, from a slightly different perspective. This is how the Unveiling is laid out too.

Many people have stumbled into confusion about this revelation because of thinking it to be a linear unfolding of but one plot. There are three completely distinct sections that the Revelation of Jesus is broken up into. It begins with the ***first sequence* (Rev. 1:1 - 3:22)**, in which things are approached from the perspective of *Jesus' judgment of the church*. It then reloads in the second ***sequence* (Rev 4:1 - 11:19)**, in which things are now approached from the perspective of Jesus *judging the nations*. And finally, the ***third sequence* (Rev. 12:1- 22:21)** reloads again and unfolds from the perspective of Jesus *judging the Beast and his false prophet, Babylon and Satan, along with the rebellious dead, the place of the dead (Hades/hell)*, and ultimately, *death itself.*

Okay, you now have some understanding of why this study is structured the way it is. Now let's look at Jesus, in His unveiling.

THE PURPOSE OF THIS BOOK

Here is the theme I hope you will see in the Unveiling;

1. Our species originally had harmony with God, with Nature, and thus with ourselves that we no longer have. This harmony looked like us feeling loved and provided for by God. It is this loss of harmony that is responsible for our species' dysfunction, for our destructive chaos. This disharmony manifested as a change in us having a relationship with a God of unconditional love to one in which we have to function well for God to love and provide for us.

2. That Jesus, and the divine forgiveness He represents, is the cure for disharmony and thus also the psychological dysfunction that results from disharmony.

3. Jesus means for us to suffer with him, and he does because the suffering that is brought to bear by love frees us from the tyranny that fear wields over our life (in our destructive compulsive, and obsessive behavior).

The most basic aspect of suffering is that it is something we experience without us having any cognitive, conscientious control over it whatsoever. The only resource we have to survive suffering is that one resource we are generally most afraid to utilize, our autonomous unconscious mind (our spiritual self), and by extension, God. *{Autonomous means our unconscious mind has a mind of its own, operating independently from our cognitive mind,}* Our unconscious mind is our spiritual self. We have lost a harmonious connection with it precisely to the same degree we have lost a harmonious connection with God.

This loss is symbolically represented as God closing off access to the tree of life to our species after the fall. All that God would speak to us must originate in our spiritual self. Even our ability to accept miracles that happen in front of our eyes, like the ability to effectively grasp divinely authored scripture must come from a harmonious connection with our unconscious mind. It is the channel through which God communicates to our cognitive mind.

All wisdom/insight, creativity, conviction, healing, and love are generated by God in the unconscious mind and delivered whole to the cognitive mind. Our reasoning cognitive mind cannot generate insight, love, or creativity. The words God must speak to us in order to restore our being to full function will only come to our cognitive mind via our unconscious mind, our spiritual self. And our species has come to be as unjustly afraid of it as it is of God.

All of our intellectual arrogance is completely worthless in bringing about the cessation of that suffering over which we have no control. That is why God deploys suffering. We, humans, are manically driven by subjective fears and counterproductive pride to seek control over pain. The fear and pride-driven solutions we so intellectually deploy only ever add to our new list of problems. They never lessen them.

It is Jesus and the restoration of the awareness that we are absolutely loved by God (because of His forgiveness of us via Jesus's sacrifice for the sins of the world) that makes it possible for us to trust both God and His spiritual connection with us (the autonomous unconscious mind). Without Jesus, we will never have a harmonious connection with God or our spiritual self, and we will never get the restoration we need from God through this spiritual connection with God.

The *Unveiling/the Revelation of Jesus truly* is an unveiling of Jesus. It is meant to strengthen our faith in Jesus to redeem and consecrate, to restore us, first, to harmony with God, and then to restore us to working order. This unveiling of Jesus is not primarily about the end of the world. Instead, it very powerfully reveals HOW Jesus restores what's been damaged...

1. in us,
2. in human society around us, and
3. in the universe as a whole.

The Unveiling should leave you greatly emboldened to follow Jesus wherever He leads you, and through whatever pain and sorrow He will lead you. The transformation we need to undergo is to have our trusting harmony with God restored to us. Without this trust, we are not capable of being natural or functional humans.

One of the main strategies our soul's enemy, pride/Satan employs to sabotage our trust in God is to make us feel bad about ourselves for undergoing the suffering Jesus leads His followers through. After we have been made to feel bad, we can no longer see that it is Jesus who has been leading us into this suffering and out the other side into empowerment. Instead, we view our damaged selves as being the origin of all our suffering. This induces us to abort the spiritual life, the trusting relationship with God we have begun living out. The *Unveiling of Jesus* will counter that evil strategy most wonderfully. It will show us just how central Jesus is to the full restoration of our relationship with God.

Everything in this artificial, broken world culture we all were raised in urges us to manically build a life that is free from pain. So, when Jesus leads us into suffering, we inevitably feel like losers, like social failures. We in the Christian community have not yet fully trusted Jesus to be our acceptability to God and to restore our damaged life. Consequently, we too, have come to think that Christian life is merely about building up our level of comfort and ease by getting good things from God. As a result, when we follow Jesus into suffering, we inevitably feel like losers, even in our Christian communities, and it is no small thing to find oneself in the out-group of one's religious community. God made us herd animals after all.

Our being without the security and comfort of a social herd is naturally an immense hardship for us.

Hopefully, in reading through this book you will begin to grasp just how wonderful the level of change is that Jesus means to bring into our broken lives and come to truly count it all joy when you suffer with Jesus.

Our restored status with God is a finished work. NOTHING else needs to be done about that. Now Jesus will make use of this viable connection we have with God (using this awareness of our acceptance) to lead us into the training/the discipline we need for our wounded hearts to be able to trust God/and by extension, trust nature, completely. Trust is the basis for harmony between sentient beings. Without the ability to trust God we cannot live out a harmonious connection with God, and our existence will reflect that disharmony in all the dysfunction that results from disharmony.

Jesus is not dead. God raised him from the dead, and he even appeared to and physically lived for a time with his followers after his crucifixion. This is important for us to understand because Jesus is intent on shepherding his followers today.

He wants us to follow him. *Jesus wants us to follow him.* I cannot say this often enough. We cannot ponder this often enough; Jesus wants us to follow him, not just accept that He existed. He is there in your life if you have believed in his sacrifice for your sins. He is waiting for you to want his leading in your life, to pursue his involvement in your life.

Following Jesus is not about intellectually reading the bible and intellectually applying it to your life, and then pasting Jesus' label on your knowledge after the fact. This is following your own understanding (which the bible warns us against doing-*Proverbs 3:5*). Following Jesus is deeding your entire life to Jesus so that you no longer have a right to say what Jesus does with your life. Following Jesus is trusting the reality that NOTHING you encounter in life is other than Jesus' shepherding of your soul. This kind of dependency will lead you to constantly ask him what he is doing in your life through circumstances (often painful ones), and why he is doing it. I can tell you from a lifetime of this kind of life with Jesus, that He ***will tell you,*** and that will leave you feeling way more at peace and healed than you do if you run your life.

Very often, he will tell you what he is doing in your life by leading you to read a passage in the Bible. You will see a metaphor for what he is doing there, or you will be given some encouragement from some biblical principle or concept to continue trusting in His love and guidance. This is a big part of what he meant by giving us to eat of the tree of life.

You may come to see, in reading this book, just how lovely the experience of meeting Jesus in the bible is to me. An intimate rendezvous with God in the Bible is an exquisite pleasure. I hope you come to have this experience with God. However, you will not get to do so if you read the bible hoping to merely analytically learn principles by which to self-righteously run your life.

God means to govern your life, so you must seek Him, seek intimacy with Him, and love from Him. God will lead you to meet up with Him in the Bible. He really did author the bible and did so for this purpose.

The history of our species is full of examples of people who have clung to their purely intellectual understanding of scripture (The religious leaders that had Jesus crucified come to mind). Clinging to God instead requires us to let go of our confidence in our understanding of Scripture. You cannot have two masters. You will love one and hate the other, as Jesus said. We will either trust in our understanding of the bible, or trust in God, but not both.

There is a deeply entrenched conflict in humanity. This is a conflict between a self-righteous trust in ourselves and a humble trust in God. Our trust in our understanding of scriptures is but one form of us trusting in ourselves. Jesus will preside over the death of our trust in our human resources, and deliver us to that land of rest in God's resources. That deliverance, of both the heart of believers and the heart of collective humanity, is wonderfully depicted for us in the Unveiling of Jesus.

Here comes the Judge!

His judgment will deliver us from bondage to our distrust in God. All power and authority have been given to Jesus to resolve this trust issue in our species. Man will cling to his prideful trust in his resources to the very end. But Jesus (and that means that what Jesus represents as the divine creative force and divine forgiveness of our sins) is divinely appointed and empowered to govern, to judge/to restore our problematic humanity. God's judgment is always healing for those that accept it and is destruction for those that don't. Divine forgiveness will creatively restore everything broken in us if we follow it without stipulation.

We can justifiably say the same thing about nature. Those that won't embrace the reality of the causes and effects of nature will be destroyed by those effects. Those that embrace the reality of those causes and effects will learn to adjust in constructive ways that provide healing and thriving.

Jesus - divine forgiveness presides over an everlasting kingdom. He crushes to powder all the kingdoms – all the governance of men. Human kingdoms represent all efforts by humanity, by our subjective and progressively dysfunctional cognitive mind to rule our troublesome humanity. And this kingdom of Jesus will never end. Glory to God! Hallelujah!

CHAPTER 1 – JESUS JUDGES THE ECCLESIA

Rev. 1:1-12 Introduction to Jesus' Judgment on the Ecclesia

First, I need to tell you something about what I am going to do in applying my commentary on chapter 1 of Revelation. I will post the first verse and then I will add a long section of commentary on this verse that also includes some cultural and historical context for the things dealt with in the Revelation of Jesus. In particular, I have injected a section on fertility cults, which were all the idols that the bible references. You will need to see that fertility cults are devoted to self-righteous productivity to see that Jesus is the antidote to them. He will ultimately embody in His followers the God-given alternative to human-derived productivity, which the bible refers to as the life of the Spirit.

Most of the commentary on the following verses will be of much shorter length. I just felt the need to give you some contextual information before going further with this book.

(Revelation 1:1) The Revelation of Jesus Christ, which God gave Him to show unto His servants, even the things which must shortly come to pass:

People differ over whether this passage reads; the revelation given *to Jesus* or the *revelation of Jesus*. Since Jesus was a human, with all of the natural limitations of a human being, he would not know what God is yet to do unless God told Him. Jesus said; **(Mat 24:36)'** *No one knows the day (not even the Son) except God."* So, whether this revelation is given *to* Jesus or given about Jesus, it is an unveiling *of* He who resolves all rebellion, all disharmony, in the universe. God gives Jesus this revelation about how His destiny will unfold just as He gives Him the scroll of judgment to unroll and implement. And Jesus gives this information about Him to us who follow Him.

The fact that Jesus is seen receiving this message implies He has been given God's authority to rule the affairs of men and the affairs of this universe. The psychological significance of Jesus ruling the universe is that this *Jesus*-reality now governs the destiny of man. The prideful self-righteous legalism of Satan had been the only ruling principle of our species. This self-righteous legalism was the original sin and is based on the performance-based-acceptance delusion Satan subtly injects into us to get us to manically govern ourselves with our subjective value system. The great conflict of our species is over who will govern our problematic human condition, God or man. Will God's Spirit (God's mentality of unconditional love) change our hearts to want what God wants or will our relying on human understanding of what constitutes good and evil behavior effectively govern our life)? And only Jesus, divine forgiveness of our sins liberates us to let go of our self-governance and trust in God's governance.

When people were in harmony with God they were in harmony with nature and thus with themselves and each other. Harmony is how we thrive. This revelation declares that Jesus is given all authority to rule God's creation by restoring and maintaining harmony with God. It implies that a rather enormous development has taken shape in the state of the spiritual universe and in the conscious life of humankind.

The human species is now collectively aware (on some level) that humanity is and was always meant to look and be like Jesus. There is a problem, however, that the idea of divine forgiveness stirs up in our minds. If there is such a thing as forgiveness, does that not contradict the idea of reaping what we sow; that choices have consequences?

Unconditional love from God does not contradict the principle that choices have consequences, because unconditional love is a part of the system of the unfolding laws of cause and effect. God is love, and so He loves us, period! Yet, because He loves us, He wants us to function well, and His laws of cause-and-effect mark where we don't function well. God's laws of cause and effect include the laws governing our species' choice-making factor.

The human species are designed to need to learn by trial and error how to function well. Thus forgiveness works together harmoniously with the laws of cause and effect in as much as it empowers us to learn, not having to worry about our errors rendering us of no value to the universe and God. Forgiveness expresses the unconditional love required for our species to learn from mistakes. If we cannot learn from our mistakes, we will reap dire consequences.

Forgiveness, then, does not contradict the karmic laws of cause and effect; it fulfills them by empowering us to live in harmony with God's design for our species. If we live our life according to the most fundamental law of all, that God is love, and that this God of love gets to express His love more fully by us having to learn how to function well *(thus placing a greater value on us than on our performance, as love would do)*, then we will reap the fruit of this sewing by learning to function well. Like the rest of Karma's laws, submission to unconditional love's forgiveness makes the human cognitive system operate effectively.

Here's the last piece of the forgiveness puzzle.

Yes, although

1. love is absolutely, and can only ever be unconditional,

2. relationships are highly conditioned on whether both parties want that relationship.

3. There is also the fact that the human species' problems with an emotionally damaged identity significantly affect how they see themselves, see God, and know what they want. Thus, how we see ourselves also determines how well we behave.

This identity problem is depicted in the Edenic story as the serpent being coopted by Satan who is the symbolic representation of pride. Pride is a damaged identity and the subjective solutions we formulate to deal with that damage. The bible's use of the serpent symbolism necessarily implies that it views this aspect of our consciousness as something good, when God makes use of it, and harmful when Satan (pride) makes use of it. Specifically, the snake represents the instinctual drive to become cognitively aware of ourselves of our identity. Our identity is constantly changing with the unfolding of our life, so we need to constantly ask who we are now. This *asking* mechanism in us is the identity instinct, the serpent. Pride is what happens when our identity instinct is coopted by a subjective, fear-driven impulse to fix the damage done to our identity.

Thus, pride is essentially us subjectively trying to cope with damage to our idea of ourselves (to our identity). This means that as our idea of ourselves changes, any destructive changes to our idea of who we are result in self-destructive changes to our objectives. And the most self-destructive objective of all is the desire to feed upon the knowledge of good and evil, in order to better our performance (and thus improve our level of acceptability.).

The desire to feed on information about what constitutes good and evil behavior is a desire born of damage to our identity. We see our value as being based upon our performance, rather than upon that which is responsible for our existence (God). The delusion of performance-based acceptance is implied in the bible's symbolism of Satan's co-opting of the God-created serpent. This co-opting is not generally understood for the damage to our identity that it represents, yet only this meaning makes the whole story resemble our human experience. Eve could not have been tempted to sin were it not for the presence of damage to her idea of herself.

The damage to our identity is expressed beautifully in the words of the Eden story's Satan co-opted serpent. *God does not want you to be like Him, knowing good and evil.* This thought could only take root in a human that had already undergone some disorienting experience with fear. Fear itself is not a sin. It is just a matter of our naturally subjective human cognition getting disoriented by the unresolved experience of pain. Fear represents damage to our identity in that it disorients us in our surroundings. Yet, because we are disoriented *(because we no longer are certain we belong to the universe we are a part of because we now think we must perform better if we are going to continue to deserve to exist)*, we are now vulnerable to the poisonous coping mechanism of pride's self-righteous legalism.

Nothing else can logically account for Mankind's seduction at a time we were said to be in total harmony with God. If we were in total harmony with God, we should have been able to see Satan's temptation for the evil it was. If we were not originally in harmony with God how can God judge us for behaving in disharmony with Him? How could God possibly judge us for falling into sin? The answer is that fear naturally disorients us, and God designed our species to learn from experience how to function well. This collective experience with fear and the disorientation it brings to our cognitive mind leaves us vulnerable to forming subjective conclusions about ourselves. And our species' long history is exactly that; it is humanity learning lies/subjective conclusions from its experience with fear and pain. It is also humanity learning from this error not to let fear's disorientation drive us into self-righteous coping. We avoid being seduced by our prideful inner serpent by turning to God for the resolution of our fears. And we must learn from experience to do this.

Only by knowing we are loved, only by us feeling totally loved, is it possible for us to totally love others. And only that choice to embrace forgiveness is effective in countering the delusion of performance-based acceptance. As Jesus put it; *he who is forgiven much, loveth much.* Divine forgiveness, essentially, heals our damaged identity. We no longer think our value comes from our good performance. Being forgiven not only removes the dysfunctional behavior from our moral credit report, but it shows us clearly that God's love for us does not depend upon our performance. Else God would not have forgiven our poor functioning, would He?

So, understand this fundamental idea; that Unconditional love is only fully expressed in a gesture of forgiveness. Choosing self-righteous legalism is based upon the delusion of performance-based acceptance. It is the one choice that results in disharmony with love, which is unconditional. It does because it chooses a prideful, compensatory idea of us over the reality of unconditional love *(that we are loved apart from our performance)*.

Sin is essentially us not trusting God to provide us with everything we need to survive and thrive, beginning with acceptance. This distrust is what breaks the harmony between God and us. It is not the mistakes we make themselves. Sin is us choosing to operate without God. It is not God choosing to stop loving us.

The New Testament's emphasis on the contrast between the Spirit and the Flesh (the Greek word for flesh is *sarx)* is all about the issue of our distrust in God to be our source of life. It never was, as is often wrongly suggested, about God not wanting us to do naughty (fleshly) things. The Greek word *sarx* etymologically means the muscles under the skin, which means it is pointing to our human strength. God wants us to depend upon the strength of His spirit, to govern and restore our damaged humanity, not our human strength/flesh/sarx.

Jesus never sinned, because Jesus was born with the undamaged harmony with God that Adam was created with, and thus with a completely healthy idea of himself. Jesus did make mistakes, but those mistakes were not generated by a damaged idea of himself. Thus, His mistakes never involved the rebellious impulse that comes from such damage. Jesus was never willfully disobedient. Rather he was just not fully clear on *how* to obey what God was wanting for him. This is why it is stated that "*He learned obedience by the things that he suffered*". Jesus too needed to be disciplined by God, that is, trained by Him. We, however, must not only be taught how to do what God wants us to do but must also be taught/be conditioned to *want* to do what God wants us to. In other words, God's parenting/His discipline of us must include the restoration of our now damaged idea of ourselves. We see this kind of discipline of our damaged identity unfolding in this unveiling of Jesus.

Making mistakes, and failing to function well do not affect our connection with God. It never has. And even our distrusting sin did not end God's love for us. It did, however, end our ability to trust in God's love, and the loss of trust in God effectively ended our harmonious connection with Him. Our embrace of the delusion of performance-based acceptance caused us to think our failures and mistakes separated us from God's love when it was our embrace of this delusion that ended our harmony with God. And this damaged idea of our place in the larger scheme of things led us to make worse and worse mistakes.

As mentioned, one can justifiably say that our sins have come to separate us from a harmonious union with God. But it must be understood that that does not mean it was our mistakes that separated us from God. Instead, it was our loss of trust in God which separated us from God. And the mistakes we do because of this distrust we have in God, then do become a sign that we are not in trusting harmony with God. It is this state of distrust that is the essential factor in separation from God. The mistakes we make because of this distrust only become judged by God as sin by association with the distrust in Him that fostered those mistakes.

Similarly, the righteousness/the harmony we have with God is essentially established by us trusting God. Yet the deeds we do because we trust in God, the deeds we do in righteousness, become judged as righteous deeds by association with the trust that generated those deeds. Even so, there is a distinction to be made between the deeds and the trust (or absence of trust) that generates our deeds.

This distinction is why there is no real conflict between the Apostle Paul stating that we are made righteous by faith, apart from works, and James stating that faith without works is dead. Yes, it is trusting God that renders us in harmony with God (renders us righteous), yet genuine trust/faith in

God will produce real changes in us. And if there are no real changes in us then we did not actually have trust/faith in God.

A self-righteous mentality in us would tell us to do works in order to prove that we genuinely have faith/trust. Yet a godly mentality in us would tell us to look to see if there have been real changes in our life, and if not, to admit that we need God to give us some genuine trust/faith in Him that we do not currently have. Each change that we need must begin with us having God-given trust/faith that God will and can make that change in us.

God will only ever accept our separation from Him if, after a lifetime of His wooing and prodding, we pride-fully cling to our delusion of Performance-Based-Acceptance, thus effectively, willfully, choosing to permanently separate ourselves from unconditional Love. God will honor the choices we make, and He will because respect for the will of another is an essential expression of love. Love needs the object of its love to have a choice (whether or not to receive that love) for it to be fully expressed. Those of us who have loved someone already know this reality about love.

God's referencing of Jesus being given authority to unfold God's scroll of healing judgment on the world implies that not only is our identity meant to be like Jesus, but also our destiny and behavior will be shaped by His trusting harmonious mentality. Again, it is said of Jesus' mentality;

"*Hebrews 5:8 though he was a Son, yet learned obedience by the things which he suffered;*

:9 and having been made perfect, he became unto all them that obey him the author of eternal salvation;".

In like manner, the human species, over the length of our history, has been learning how to obey God via the training discipline that God is collectively and individually taking us through. We are undergoing a divine course in understanding how to fulfill God's will for us and how to be fully expressed, humans. One could also say that we are all undergoing a course of psychological therapy in God's loving hands.

It is an essential aspect of the human species that we are meant to learn from our experiences (including our failures). And whereas Jesus, who was in total harmony with God, could make mistakes and learn from them, the rest of our species, as a result of the Fall, have lost the freedom to learn from our mistakes. The Jesus-gesture of divine forgiveness restores to our species the capacity to fully learn from our experiences. Without the embrace of Jesus, and all He represents, no member of our species can trust they can afford to make, and thus truly, fully, face up to their mistakes. And so, learning from those mistakes is completely beyond our reach (*except in minor circumstances in which our mistakes do not affect our identity, our idea of ourselves*).

As a species, we inwardly, and naturally, want to fulfill God's will for us (live in harmony/in righteousness with God and by extension, nature). Yet as psychologically damaged, naturally subjective human beings we just don't know how to live in trusting harmony with God or nature anymore, and won't unless and until God shows us. God shows us what he wants from and for us through Jesus' "faithful witness" (his example of trustworthy, harmonious submission to God), even to death on the cross for the sins of the world.

Whereas Jesus could embrace pain and suffering, and fulfill God's will, we find it difficult, and often impossible to embrace pain, because we associate pain with our failure and our failures with our worthlessness.

The governing principle upon which our species' consciousness is built, has been dominated by satan, by *pride* since the fall (because man had conceded it to Satan as a result of his choice to pridefully disobey God and feed upon knowledge of what constitutes good and evil human behavior). Yet this authority to rule the destiny of believers now belongs to Jesus as a result of His faithful witness and our choice to humbly trust in Him (and specifically his death and resurrection for our sins). Even so, that divine governance is progressive.

This is why Jesus is referred to as the second Adam (**1Corinthians 15:45**), and the firstborn among many brethren (**Romans 8:29**). The

Satan idea/the pride idea of our self is that which aggressively fights against the real, harmonious nature of our being.

Another way of stating this authority that Satan has had in our species is to say that our species experienced a trauma. The serpent of pride is created by the dragon, which is a metaphor for trauma, the trauma of lost harmony with God and nature. This is the dragon depicted in the Unveiling Of Jesus. This pride generated the notion that God was selfishly keeping the moral goods for himself. Some subjective experiences of pain gave us the idea that Nature//God did not want us to thrive, and perhaps didn't even want us to survive. This idea about ourselves feels like rejection by God. When we humans feel rejected, we tend to reject our rejecter. And when we feel rejected for being selfish, the selfishness that a damaged identity produces in us, we inevitably project that selfishness back on God.

We had never thought of God as being selfish until that moment, and as a result, we were rendered burdened by a fearful idea of ourselves and God. Jesus is the healing that God provided for this collective wounded identity. He replaces the compensatory coping mechanism of self-righteous legalism with a mentality of harmonious, completely trusting, son-ship with God. The healing of our identity comes simultaneously with the healing of our idea of God. We see God as being unconditionally loving, and we see ourselves as being loved.

Jesus is also referred to as the *lamb of God…* who takes away the sins of the world (John 1:29). In this biblical phrase (*the Lamb of God*) we see the metaphorical expression of an unblemished (that is, a perfectly healthy capacity for) instinctive trust in divine providence. *{Our species' long association with the lamb species is that it must depend upon our species' providence for its well-being, in exactly the way we humans were meant to depend upon God for our well-being.}*

In the *Lamb of God,* God expresses his forgiveness of our sins, while at the same time giving us a picture of what we would look like if we were sinless (that is, holding an undamaged idea of ourselves.). It is our humble embrace of the forgiveness we have in Jesus' sacrifice for our sins that allows us to embrace Jesus (*the Lamb of God archetype of trust*) as the ruling/ the governing principle in our lives. We begin to follow and trust in God and nature as we also trust in the forgiveness that we receive because of Jesus' sacrifice for us.

{The ruling principle in a person's life is that idea or truth that forms the premise of our life's goals, desires, and actions, in as much as it, more than any other idea, represents what we want out of life. We humans by our God-designed nature want a son and daughter-like connection with God and nature. Paul speaks of the spirit/the mentality of sonship we receive from Jesus. Jesus expressed this mentality in statements such as; I do nothing of myself. I do only that which is of my father. My meat is to do the will of my father. The father and I are one. etc.}

We have been born into a world culture whose governing principle is symbolized as Satan. And since symbolically, Satan is a representation of pride's rebellion, which is fear-driven and subjective, is a reactionary coping mechanism, we can say that the world culture (the world system) we are born into is a product of a fear-driven, reactionary egotism (*pride*).

This egoism manifests as a denial of the existence of any sort of universal standard of existence to which we must personally account. That is to say, our species' collective delusion leads us to believe we can force nature to accept our progressively dysfunctional existence. Less and less does it occur to mankind to become restored to good function, and so fit in more effectively with the nature we are a part of.

Fear Makes Us Unable To Trust. Pride Makes Us Not Want To. A person afraid of drowning will often not be able to trust anyone to help them. Pride, which is about our idea of ourselves being damaged, would make a person not drowning, not faced with imminent death, reject help. A lifeguard expects to have to counter a desperate need for control in a drowning victim. A lifeguard would however have to let a prideful person, whose pride is something that might lead to drowning, go on their way. This is our *divine* lifeguard's predicament.

Our not wanting to account to God is a spiritual manifestation of the psychological damage we have sustained to our identity, our idea of ourselves, and its effect on our life. This damage renders us disoriented, conceptually and emotionally disconnected from our surroundings, no longer in harmony with it and ourselves. We humans do not even see that we are a harmonious part of our universal surround. We are just that damaged.

We profess that we see ourselves as being a part of nature, but we act completely as though we aren't. We consistently come up with every kind of solution that seeks to limit or destroy that very nature we say we are a part of. We see ourselves as having to conquer nature, to overcome its tendency to wipe us out of existence. We can see no meaningful harmony with the nature we are a part of (*and that includes fellow members of the human species*), except as a consequence of the embrace of divine forgiveness. This obsessive need to conquer nature would continue unabated in us until we humans have utterly wiped out the very nature we need to exist. We are not very far from that place now.

This idea that there is no God-factor that humanity is in harmony with (and so must account to) always takes the form of human self-governance via the subjective human conscience, which ideologically, philosophically, and theologically manifests as a fixation on improving our value via improving our moral functionality.

And since if there is no God factor by which there can be the needed criteria for determining absolute value, then every suboptimal condition that exists in our species, every damaged cognitive state we have is essentially rendered moral or functional in our thoughts by emotional default. Without concepts of value, there is no meaning for anything. Eventually, and ironically, given enough time to develop fully, this rebellious embrace of subjectivity becomes a life bound by a chaotic judgment of others. This chaotic judgmentalism is a deification of one's subjective values, that invariably manifests as a life ruled by the fear-driven instinct to survive. The Will and the conscience finally become one, in a violent psychotic break. And this, apparently, is where our species is headed.

Without a viable God idea, there remains no criterion for sanity, and the insanity of fear replaces the sanity of love/of God as the foundational template for our lives. This is so because God represents the idea that love, that harmony is the factor that governs the systematic unfolding of the material universe. In other words, a viable God-idea allows for the sanity that everything is a natural and wonderful part of one harmonious system. If you cannot see that everything is a product of an ordered, systemic, unfolding (with the ordered system as an expression of love's harmony), everything begins to fall apart in our cognitive grasp.

In as much as Jesus is presented as having been empowered by God to be the ruling principle of the human species, it implies that the transformation of the human species (into a species that can once more harmoniously trust their human needs and issues to God's providence), is in the process of unfolding in us as we speak, via the idea of Love's forgiveness.

Jesus is presented as having been given the authority to rule (and thus restore) those of us humans who choose to submit to forgiveness's rule of our existence. This submission to Jesus's rule of our life looks like our continuing choice to depend upon His sacrifice for our sins to make us acceptable to God (or in psychological terms, to make us aware that we are accepted and loved by God, regardless of our failures).

The authority Jesus holds to meet out God's judgment on rebellion within His followers results from His faithful witness of perfect son-ship (via giving himself up as a sacrifice for the sins of the world). Jesus' authority to deliver God's judgment on the nations, and on the spirit realm, will in a similar way result from our faithful witness.

The faithful witness we followers of Jesus will manifest will essentially be our coming to value God more than life itself (as Jesus did). Only

then can God present solid testimony that His (sacrificial, forgiving) love can effectively govern every problem or need a human can have). Only then can God say that love fully, effectively, restores us to harmony with Him, thus justifying His judgment upon all who willfully rebel against God's governance, God's providence, via forgiveness. These rebels receiving judgment are they who essentially live out the lie that God/that love cannot be trusted to be the source of all we could ever need.

If God cannot effectively govern mankind with love (to the point of restoring him to harmony with God via love's forgiveness), then there is no basis for God to judge Satan/judge Pride. Satan could point out to God; *see, Your love was not enough to get the job done, of effectively governing/ restoring the human condition.* He would say to God; that *perhaps fear (and pride) is necessary to rule after all.*

There is a courtroom drama unfolding here and unless you understand the evidence the divine prosecuting attorney is attempting to bring forward to bring a conviction then you cannot understand this *revelation of Jesus.* This divine conviction, this proof that silences Satan, will render the entire universe restored to harmony with God.

All dysfunction in the universe is a product of Pride's rebellion and the resulting disharmony with God. To remove this rebellion from His universe God must clearly show that we creatures, who have been given free will, could have **viably chosen** harmonious submission to God, and this, even after we had fallen out of harmony with Him.

Understand This Central Theme; pride is essentially the damage done to our identity, to our idea of ourselves, and is also the things we subjectively do to counter that loss of a sense that we are loved. Knowing we are loved enables us to know we are naturally and wonderfully placed in our universal surroundings. This in turn empowers us to behave in proactive, loving ways. This contest between God (between Love, and love's forgiveness), and Pride (and pride's delusional self-righteous, performance-based-acceptance), is the drama that is being played out in the Bible and is being fully developed and completed in the Revelation of Jesus.

Here Is A Biblical Summary Of The Underlying Psychological Equation Defining Our Species Many Psychological Issues

Knowing we are loved generates good/generates functional behavior.

Pride (and the doomed idea of ourselves that pride represents) generates dysfunctional behavior.

Knowing we are loved generates trusting submission to God's will. As a result of this trusting harmony with God, we are one with nature as well.

Pride generates the need to govern our progressively worsening human behavior via the superficial and subjectively understood deployment of concepts about good and evil. We are in this way rendered at odds with nature. We humans are very busy suppressing much that is essential in a fully functioning human. This effectively renders us all obsessive and compulsive hypocrites.

In the Adam and Eve account, it is made clear that it was man's choice to govern his behavior (via the deployment of the knowledge of good and evil) that severed his original harmony with God. Before that fateful choice (to feed on the knowledge of right and wrong, good and evil) mankind knew perfect harmony with God. He was living out a completely natural existence, with no hypocrisy, no suppression, no obsession, and no compulsion.

When he needed to act, he simply did what he wanted, and what he wanted was to do whatever his father (God) wanted him to do. He felt a strong closeness with this spiritual core of his existence. **He did not ever need to know if what he was contemplating doing was right or wrong!** He only cared if it was what his Father wanted.

By opting for the legalistic self-governance of Pride, humanity lost harmony with the spiritual core of his being, and this disharmony, this spiritual leaven quickly permeated his whole existence. We put our trust in the knowledge of right and wrong as the basis for making good choices, instead of trusting in God to guide us on the paths of harmony/righteousness with Him. Instead of simply doing what He wanted us to do, what He spiritually motivated, instructed, and empowered us to do (by His speaking to us via our autonomous unconscious mind/our spiritual self). We have become a species of compulsive, obsessive, fear-driven, hypocrites.

(Romans 8:14 **For as many as are led by the Spirit of God, these are sons of God.***)*

By simply accepting that we are in a state of dysfunction, because of being in an inherited state of rebellious disharmony with God and nature, and then accepting His forgiveness for our rebellion and resulting dysfunction, we effectively are brought back into a state of harmonious submission to God's and nature's rule. We are restored to son and daughter-ship with God.

If you are from India, you might say it this way. By accepting that we are in a state of dysfunction, because of being in a state of broken harmony with God we also distrust and are at odds with karma. By accepting His forgiveness for our distrustful distance from Him, and the resulting dysfunction, we effectively are progressively brought back into a state of harmony with God and with the laws of karma.

God first resolves our disharmony with Him, and then He resolves our problems that resulted from this disharmony using the Jesus arch-example/ archetype/this Jesus avatar if you will, of divine forgiveness.

And when that historic moment comes for God to judge all of prideful, rebellious mankind, He will have already previously offered mankind divinely restored submissive harmony with Him, via forgiveness. Even so, that population of humans, who humbly do accept this gesture of loving forgiveness, will also first need God to heal the emotional dysfunction within them that has accrued in our species and been passed on to each of us since the fall. This is necessary for God to have the testimony, the proof

He is looking for to proceed with judging the rebellion still present within the rest of mankind.

God uses this same Jesus-arch-example of trusting harmony *(only now this arch-example includes the faithful witness of Jesus's followers)* to clearly show what rebellious mankind could have done, but chose not to. This expression of trusting harmony with God becomes the testimony (the evidence) God the prosecutor is looking for to show that those who elected to refuse harmony with God did have a viable alternative to their prideful self-righteousness.

After all, it is only a lack of trust in, a lack of harmony with God that manifests as every sort of dysfunction known to man. Because we don't trust God to be the origin of our life's productivity we make (like the idolaters of previous civilizations) a **god** out of the life we naturally need, and in the process must co-dependently sacrifice some innocent aspect of our human existence to this false god's veneration. In other words, our idiolatry is a metaphorical representation of our compulsive desires and obsessive emotions, and the emotional wounds that drive those obsessions and compulsions.

Contemporary human sacrifice looks like us being a *work-a-holic*, it looks like us sacrificing our relationships with those who should be precious to us, to fulfill a mission or a goal. It looks like us sacrificing the resolution of, and the fulfillment of our own emotional needs in order for us to pride-fully maintain our focus on our mission, vision, or goal. It looks like us suppressing all manner of natural instinctual and emotional human existence to render us morally whole beings. It manifests in our suppression of the individual we are so that we can be approved of by our social herd. Thus, idols represent the stuff we destructively do because we cannot trust God to provide life for us.

Fertility Cults and the Revelation of Jesus

Fertility cults, psychologically speaking, represent a codependent relationship with nature as well as with God. One believes he must help nature/help god to help him by doing something unnatural that will induce nature/god to meet our need for fertility, for a full life.

{Codependence is essentially that kind of relationship in which one party in the relationship does not share responsibility for the well-being of the relationship with their partner and instead takes all of the responsibility for the well-being of the relationship upon themself.}

This codependency with gods and goddesses invariably manifests as distrust in nature to give us all we need to survive and thrive. We no longer believe that God/Gods/goddesses/or nature truly want to give us what we need. Thus, we must sacrifice needed aspects of our life, to get them to meet our needs. It is this almost universal underlying mentality of mankind's relationship with the gods that was so hateful to the Bible's God of love.

Without this concept of the bible's treatment of the conflict between codependency and unconditional love, the God of the bible appears to be nothing but a petty, spiteful, insecure deity, full of rage and pride. In other words, He looks pretty much like the rest of our specie's gods and goddesses. Yet the Bible's God is very much not like them, is singular in being a representation of unconditional love. And the fact that this is so is strikingly significant.

Food is but one sort of productivity we humans can't trust God for any more. There are also gods of safety, prosperity, reproduction, power, self-realization, independence, interdependence, fitting into our social herd, purity, etc. Pretty much anything we humans instinctually need we make a god of it. The reality though is that all instinctual human needs, and thus also, all idols, come in two categories;

Obsessive, compulsive needs, or *gods*, of

    1. **Safety**/Survival

and

    2. **Productivity**/Prosperity/Fertility

In other words, we humans are fixated, out of fear, on our need for survival and production.

Are you driven by fear to be found acceptable? Then you will be compulsively defensive. Are you fixated on your need to avoid the pain of rejection? Then you will become compulsive in your need to keep a low profile, out of your massive need for acceptance, thus perpetuating the very wounding that you want to avoid. Are you fixated on your need to avoid the pain of betrayal and abandonment? Then you will become compulsive in your desire for control, thus perpetuating the very abandonment by people you wanted desperately to avoid. These fear-driven needs are all gods of safety, and they turn what is essentially a natural and good instinctual need in us into a highly self-destructive impulse. And ironically, these coping mechanisms, the veneration of these gods **always** result in the loss of the very thing we are trying to ensure we have.

Are you driven by fear to be spiritually mature, morally whole, and financially prosperous, have a high social status, be creative, industrious, or be able to have children? These fear-driven desires are all gods of productivity. Are you driven to fixate upon your need for moral integrity? Then you will be compulsively driven to be a hypocrite, thus destroying any integrity you might still have left. Are you fixated upon your need for prosperity? Then you will become compulsive in your pursuit of prosperity, thus removing from you all capacity for getting gratification from whatever prosperity you have.

The herd instinct-god makes us sell out who we are to fit in with the herd, and then we are, the real us is, already after the fact lost to the herd.

The power-god makes us sacrifice the well-being of our relationships to get power, and when we get it, we cannot ever really feel like we have it, because we originally wanted power to see to the well-being of relationships. This power instinct-god is the same god as the god of control. We lust for control, and when we get control, we have lost the safety and/or happiness we thought control would give us because it has cost us our relationships.

We make a god out of having and keeping a family, and that makes us work overtime to force the family to be what we wanted in a family, and in the process, we lose the love of everyone in our family (who wants their own unique set of things from family life).

The reason for bringing this up is that the contrast between God and *the gods* is a topic that is essential to understanding the bible and this revelation of Jesus. In the statements that Jesus makes to each of the *ecclesias* (the communities of followers and believers in Jesus), the fertility cults of the time are referenced as either being something embraced by or tolerated by the double-minded, or else they were destructive idolatrous impulses that bad leaders sewed into their poorly run communities and had to be endured by the single-minded, trusting servants of Jesus.

And throughout the entire unveiling of Jesus, the thing that fertility cults symbolize is the particular thing that God is judging in mankind (mankind's inability to trust in God for what he needs to survive and thrive, and what he does instead of trusting in God's providence). To only see the very real literal meaning of the idolatry of early Christians is to entirely miss its relevance to us, contemporary Christians. Their ancient society's deities were perfect metaphors for our species' distrust in God's love and providence.

Fertility cults, such as Baal and Ashtoreth, Bacchus and Venus, Ishtar, Astarte, Aphrodite, Dionysus, Melquart, Inanna, etc. are centered on compulsively doing some service to the *gods*. These deities are essentially our species' fear-driven coping mechanisms, our pride, deployed to ensure our fertility (our productivity) or our survival.

In pagan cultures, if it was merely ordinary productivity that was needed, then the service to the gods often took the form of the magic rite of sacred sexual intercourse (usually between temple prostitutes and those wanting productivity, and sometimes manifesting in the veneration of the ritual of **Hieros Gamos**, in which the king and the priestess either had actual ritualized sex once a year or simulated sex.). And if there was some calamity that was threatening one's existence, then service to these gods sometimes involved a magic rite of a blood sacrifice, including for many cultures, human sacrifice, or even child sacrifice. Yet sacrificial veneration always was payment for the deity's love and providence, very much like a prostitute has to pay with her sexual services for her client's providence.

The Gods Of Pride Cost Us Everything Precious To Us and Render Us Compulsively Desiring Things.

The God Of Love Provides Everything Precious To Us And Liberates Us From Our Connection With Our Compulsive Desires For Things.

It is our compulsive desire for things that causes our species so much trouble. The contrast between those gods of codependency and the God of love is THE pivotal reality our species needs to get for us to be restored to full functionality. This was not merely some subjective preference for one's own deity at work in the bible's handling of the topic of idolatry. It was pointing to a very real psychological issue in our species. Unresolved pain renders us susceptible to the coping mechanisms of pride. And when we feel loved, altruistic, proactive generosity is generated. We have been wrong in our assessment of the Bible's approach to idolatry, as merely advocating for the Bible's religion, or as it being the manifestation of an ancient people's insecure dogmatism.

The contrast to this sort of relationship with a pride *deity* is wonderfully depicted in the covenant between Abram and YHWH. Abram, who we are very poignantly told, was infertile (or his wife was), which is significant in a discussion about productivity. So, God promised him that he would make him *the father of many nations*. God's contract with Abram stipulated that God would be (would supply) Abram's prosperity and safety/*be his shield and his very great reward*. And the only thing required of Abram for God to do this was that he had to circumcise himself and his male children. This is significant just because it is such a contrast to the codependent rituals of every fertility cult.

Fertility cults required their adherents to induce the gods to provide for them by making gifts to them. These gifts were an aspect of our productivity. We could make God give us what we wanted by offering god our productivity. Abram/Abraham, by contrast, had to cut off his trust in his drive to be productive. Circumcision of the foreskin is a metaphorical way of saying, judging/letting go of your self-covering. Your trust in yourself must go.

A covering is a symbolic picture of what we trust in. In other words, to have a harmonious relationship with God (in which God would be his source of surviving and thriving), Abraham had to stop trusting in his productivity. In fertility cults, the idea was that in order for us to get what we needed from life, from God, we must fixate on what we wanted at the expense of other things we needed. This kind of fixation (along with what such a fixation costs us) is the sacrifice we give to the gods for their favors.

What God was requiring of Abraham was that he stop fixating (covering himself). In Paul's letter to the Corinthian followers of Jesus (**1 Corinthians 11:6-15**) he equates a covering with authority/authorship/origin. God did not ask Abram to castrate himself, but rather just asked that he judge/cut off from himself his self-covering, his self-authoring. He was to cut off from himself his trust in his drive to be the origin of his safety and prosperity.

There were, and still are today in the fertility cults that survive into our era, rituals to fixate on, to venerate the human organs of fertility. Veneration of Lingam and Yoni, Phallus and Vulva, is a universal religious thing. Abraham's God offered Abraham a partnership with Him, in which He, God, would be the source of everything Abraham might ever need. God was saying to Abraham, I will be everything you need if you just commit yourself to stop all your fear-driven, prideful, self-righteous, codependent attempts at inducing me to meet your needs.

And this *stopping* was mirrored in so many of the laws of Moses too, the Sabbath and the tithes, and the resting of the land, etc. This stopping of our manic, codependent activity was the rest God metaphorically provided in the Land of promise. It is a HUGE theme in the Bible, both in the Old and New Testaments. God WILL bring us to a place where we can thrive when we fully trust Him to love and provide for us all that we need. Consider this; if we cannot trust God, and by extension, nature to provide for us all we need, then we must adversely change nature to supply what we need. Can anything good ever come from doing that?

Either we will choose to sacrifice precious aspects of our lives to gain the life we need, or we will have to sacrifice/ circumcise our neurotic trust in ourselves and trust God's love instead to be the source of the productivity and survival we need. We cannot have it both ways.

ON THE EQUATING OF A COVERING WITH THAT WHICH IS THE ORIGIN OF THINGS

1 Corinthians 11:6 For if a woman is not veiled, let her also be shorn: but if it is a shame to a woman to be shorn or shaven, let her be veiled.

:7 For a man indeed ought not to have his head veiled, for as much as he is the image and glory of God: but the woman is the glory of the man.

:8 For the man is not of the woman; but the woman of the man:

:9 for neither was the man created for the woman; but the woman for the man:

:10 for this cause ought the woman to have a sign of authority on her head, because of the angels.

:11 Nevertheless, neither is the woman without the man, nor the man without the woman, in the Lord.

:12 For as the woman is of the man, so is the man also by the woman; but all things are of God.

:13 Judge ye in yourselves: is it seemly that a woman pray unto God unveiled?

:14 Doth not even nature itself teach you, that, if a man have long hair, it is a dishonor to him?

:15 But if a woman have long hair, it is a glory to her: for her hair is given her for a covering.

The idea of Authority carries embedded within it the idea that it is that which authors, or originates. Whatever we see as being the source of something is that which we trust to obtain that thing. If we view ourselves as being the source of productivity, we correspondingly put our trust in ourselves to provide this productivity to ourselves. This self-trust is the very essence of idolatry. It stems from a collective traumatic event in which we lost our harmony (and thus our trust in) the spiritual core of our existence (God). In psychological terms, it is a misguided trust in our cognitive (deductive) mind to cognitively, deductively be the source of every solution to every problem we have, instead of trusting our unconscious (spiritual) mind (and by extension, God) to generate what we need to resolve issues.

And as the apostle Paul made clear, Jesus (the idea and fact of divine forgiveness) is the symbolic representation of circumcision of our mind. Thus, our acceptance of our trust in Jesus' sacrifice is the act of circumcision that effectively puts to death our trust in our efforts to make ourselves spiritually, and morally productive.

Philippians 3:3 for we are the circumcision, who worship by the Spirit of God, and glory in Christ Jesus, and have no confidence in the flesh:

Colossians 2:11 in whom ye were also circumcised with a circumcision not made with hands, in the putting off of the body of the flesh, in the circumcision of Christ;

:12 having been buried with him in baptism, wherein ye were also raised with him through faith in the working of God, who raised him from the dead.

In Jesus' addresses to his ecclesia, he is directing his followers to confirm their salvation/their soul-circumcision, by rejecting fertility-cult-like acts of self-righteous legalism.

Magical spells, and fertility cult rituals, are used as a metaphor here for legalism. Magic *is* wholly codependent and legalistic. It depends upon man finding some secret formula, and then correctly deploying it. It panders to our trust in ourselves to be the source of what we need. In the Christianity of our day, this sort of witchcraft might look like a human-generated name-it-and claim it theology, like positive thinking, or like an application of the bible that is directed by human understanding alone, instead of God's spirit. This approach makes it as though the bible was some sort of manual for our life that we could arbitrarily deploy to get what we want; very much like a magic spell. It depends upon us, not God.

Contemporary magic might look like the arrogant legalistic dependence upon our subjective values and willpower to resolve all issues. Legalism is essentially a more contemporary form of prideful rebellion, witchcraft, of fertility Cult rituals.

Thus, it becomes evident that what Jesus is judging, concerning fertility cult worship, IS LEGALISM! And Jezebel is a symbolic reference to the church teachers who militantly teach legalism. They operate under the authority of the leaders of the Church leaders. Those church leaders who supported these teachers of legalism were metaphorically associated with King Ahab, the wife of Jezebel.).

And when there is a social environment in which legalism is present, there will often be personality cult leaders too. Most Astarte's come with a Baal. The Nicolaitans preached to their followers the abdication of their direct intimate relationship with God to a person they considered to be spiritually superior to them. This personality-cult phenomenon only happens because our sense of our acceptability with God has already been eroded in us by the presence of legalism.

And finally, Jesus also judges the mercenary selfishness of church leaders, who, like the prophet Balaam, are only serving Jesus' flock out of self-serving motives, such as the emotional need for social validation, or out of our need for financial security.

In this Revelation of Jesus, we see Jesus resolving/judging every one of these inabilities in humankind to trust God to be the source of their productivity and safety and wholeness, etc., and he begins this judgment in his own house first. And we all truly need it! We are all just as human, just as damaged by Adam's fall from harmony with God as the next person. As Isaiah put it; Isaiah 53:6

All we like sheep have gone astray; we have turned every one to his own way, and the LORD hath laid on him the iniquity of us all.

We, humans, are all iniquitous/wicked/highly damaged beings. In contemporary terms iniquity would be expressed this way; we have all been groomed (conditioned) by unresolved experiences of pain to cling to our enemy, a damaged identity/pride, and thus also to the misbehavior this generates in us. We not only do not know what we should do, naturally would do, but we also do not want to do what we should do because of the conditioning effects of our experiences with unresolved pain.

Now, it must be grasped that all of this divine judgment on the whole human population takes place in a prescribed time known as the Last Days (the time in which we see the ending of this age of disrupted harmony with God). The concluding, or "Last days" began with the coming of the Messiah *(see* **1Pe 1:20** *who was foreknown indeed before the foundation of the world, but was manifested at* **the end of times** *for your sake,).*

With the coming of Jesus and, specifically, His death and resurrection (*His faithful witness*), God's judgment on rebellion and, thus, God's restoration of harmony, has spiritually officially begun. The unfolding of this restoration judgment (via Jesus) will now commence in:

first, the judgment on the rebellion within Jesus' Body,

then the judgment on the rebellion within the nations, and

finally, Jesus' judgment on the rebellion within the spiritual entities we know as the Beast (*the collective psychosis* **within** *mankind* which is essentially the mentality of mankind's prideful hatred of the idea that God must and will save us, which is also referred to as the antichrist), and Jesus judgment on Babylon (the collective heart, the collective neurotic *values*, and culture of self-righteous-legalism), and Jesus's judgment on

Satan (the mentality of prideful rebellion against God, which generates the heart of faithless legalism).

The expression, "*Last Days*" is a reference to the conclusion of this present age in which disharmony has existed in God's otherwise harmonious universe. The events that Jesus' judgment will unfold (during the time referred to here as "***shortly coming to pass***"), is a reference to Daniel's prophecy (**see directly below**).

This cryptic phrase, "***shortly coming to pass***"(Rev 1:1), is a key left at the front door of this prophecy. What we see in this key *at the front door* is that God is signaling that pivotal moment ("*shortly*") as the time in which God would "***break in pieces the power of the Holy people***".

Daniel's Prophecy

And one said to the man clothed in linen, who was above the waters of the river, How long shall it be to the end of these wonders? And I heard the man clothed in linen, who was above the waters of the river when he held up his right hand and his left hand unto heaven, and sware by him that liveth forever that it shall be for a time, times, and a half; and when they have made an end of breaking in pieces the power of the holy people, all these things shall be finished. And I heard, but I understood not: then said I, O my lord, what shall be the issue of these things? And he said, Go thy way, Daniel; for the words are shut up and sealed till the time of the end. (Dan. 12:6-9)

What is the event that signals this "***breaking***"? It is the destruction of the Temple. This toppling of the temple served as God's **way** of triggering the coming dispersion of His people. The destruction of the temple served as the actual historical catalyst for God's "*breaking in pieces the power of the holy people*". Israel's nationhood was thereafter effectively abandoned until 1948.

So, that which was shortly to *come to pass* was not the beginning of the last days; the last days began with the first coming of Jesus. What was shortly to come to pass was the fulfillment of the events foretold in Daniel's prophecy, the beginning of Jesus's judgment upon the nations, beginning with the nation of Israel (the breaking in pieces of its power).

This did, in fact, happen shortly after John wrote that line. The time focused upon in this Revelation is this time between the destruction of the Temple in Jerusalem and the coming cataclysmic judgment of the world.

This time of judgment on the nations, which opens with the coming of the Messiah, begins with diaspora and will culminate in a great time of trouble and the outpouring of the wrath of God. And this diaspora was triggered by the destruction of the temple in Jerusalem, which unfolded roughly in John's time.

All of these events, including the Diaspora, are foretold in the Revelation of Jesus given to John.

OVERVIEW OF THE UNVEILING OF JESUS

INTRODUCTION TO THE UNVEILING OF JESUS Revelation 1:1-8 is God's introduction to the entire revelation.

SUBSECTION 1 Revelation 1:9-20 is God's introduction to the first sub-section; **Jesus Judges the ecclesia (the followers of Jesus).**

SUBSECTION 2 Revelation chapters 4 and 5 are God's introduction to the second sub-section; **Jesus judges the Nations**.

SUBSECTION 3 And Revelation 12:1-2 is God's introduction to the third sub-section; **Jesus judges Satan, Babylon, death and Hades, and the souls of the damned**.

In each of the three subsections, God introduces them by first giving us an expression of the harmony that prevails in His Kingdom. **In Jesus' judgment on the ecclesia**, we are shown Jesus, our High Priest, perfectly, harmoniously, serving in God's temple, and thus holding the pastors of the ecclesia and their flock in His hand (which metaphorically is to say, taking responsibility for their restoration).

In Jesus' judgment on the nations, we first see God portrayed, in His throne room, in perfect harmony with Himself. We are shown that Jesus, the Lamb of God, is the full expression of God's harmony with Himself (with love), and then we are shown Jesus judging the disharmony with God embodied in the nations.

Finally, in Jesus' judgment of Satan, the Beast and his false prophet, Babylon, His judgment on Hades (the place of the dead), and on Death itself, and the souls of the rebellious, we see God first portraying the fully pregnant woman of God, in labor, about to give birth to the Messiah (the man-child), who is the faithful witness, who because of His perfect trusting submission to God, is given authority by God to rule/to discipline the nations with a rod of iron.

God is showing us that His judgments are pure, just, and meted out without any ulterior motives. And proof of this purity of judgment is that God has made His wife, the woman of Revelation 12 (those humans that trust in Him, as opposed to those that don't, who prostitute themselves to their false gods) pure in her relationship with Him. And He has done this by the sacrifice of Himself on a Roman execution stake, in the person of Jesus, the Messiah. I love this about God; He did not have to tell us that about His judgment. He could have, in arrogance ignored our subjective need to have Him spell out for us that our fears that He might be like us (petty, spiteful, and bred in insecurity) are unfounded, but He condescends to our emotional needs and tells us straight out; My Judgments are pure altogether.

Praise God! Holy, Holy, Holy (fully committed... fully committed...fully committed) is God!

(Revelation 1:1-3) The Revelation of Jesus Christ, which God gave him to show unto his servants, even the things which must shortly come to pass: and he sent and

signified it by his angel unto his servant John; who bare witness of the word of God, and of the testimony of Jesus Christ, even of all things that he saw. Blessed is he that readeth, and they that hear the words of the prophecy, and keep the things that are written therein: for the time is at hand.

Please understand that this revelation, *this unveiling of Jesus* is no small matter. In being given the big picture of the total restoration of harmony in God's universe in the hands of Jesus we are confirmed in our subjective (and still in need of persuasion) human souls that God can fix what we broke in ourselves. The reason we are given this revelation is that for us to have the strength to suffer with Jesus, thus experiencing God's healing restoration of our damaged identity, and thus also fulfilling our destiny as Christ's Body and Bride, we will need to see just how potent Jesus is.

And more than that, that God really does mean to fix us. We have a very strong tendency to believe God wants us to fix ourselves. Seeing this entire prophecy about how Jesus is authorized to fix what mankind has broken, and how He is authorized to begin with fixing His church as God's high priest holding the menorah in God's temple, and finally seeing Him actually doing this fixing in the seven churches being addressed in the Book of Revelation, we are encouraged to trust Him to fix us.

And, Jesus is presented in the Unveiling as not only buying *us back for God* (as God's priests and kings), but He also redeems the entire universe. In other words, this revelation of Jesus shows us that Jesus is God's judgment on all disharmony in the universe:

- within the ecclesia (in terms of His judgment upon our self-righteous legalism);

- within the nations (in terms of His judgment on their rebellion against God's rule); and

- within the spiritual realm (in terms of His judgment on the pride of Babylon, the Beast, and Satan, and upon the fruit of that pride, of death, Hades, and the damned).

With this in mind, it is important to understand that this Revelation is primarily about Jesus, and secondarily about the things that are shortly *to come to pass*. Those who read and stand watch over the things that are written within, guarding the precious value of these things against being lost or destroyed, will be blessed because, again, the time mentioned within this revelation is at hand (i.e., they are close enough to touch, they are here).

As my suggestion (that the "*shortly come to pass*" expression is a reference to Daniel. 12:8, 9) indicates this necessarily shows that this time would begin within the lifetime of John. This is a problem for most students of this Revelation because they view the things referred to in this revelation as having not occurred yet.

To fix the apparent conflict with historical facts, they attempt to wrestle hopelessly unfounded meanings from John's wording here. Jesus meant that the things revealed herein (specifically the time in which these things happen) would shortly come to pass and, in case you didn't understand that, he confirms this assertion by saying, "*for the time is at hand*". It is already here.

So how can we link up what is written within the Unveiling with what we know of history? Well, a new interpretation of the things written within is required. I mean to suggest that when this revelation is correctly understood, it will be clear that indeed, *these things were* at hand. They did *BEGIN* at the time this revelation was given. And those followers of Jesus, those who suffered for their testimony that Jesus is the Messiah, our savior, and King, did get the blessing they needed for them to be able to fulfill their testimony of Jesus, in suffering and even death.

This is a rather significant fact for us to get, in as much as the period that began around the time John received this revelation (in about 70- 95 AD) is still in the process of unfolding, and many of the significant events of this divinely appointed time are yet to unfold. This means that we too will have our time of suffering and, for many of us, even death to endure, and so will also need what is contained in the Unveiling of Jesus.

Our Destiny (our course) as Followers of Jesus

And when he opened the fifth seal, I saw underneath the altar the souls of them that had been slain for the word of God, and for the testimony which they held: and they cried with a great voice, saying, How long, O Master, the holy and true, dost thou not judge and avenge our blood on them that dwell on the earth? And there was given them to each one a white robe; and it was said unto them, that they should rest yet for a little time until their fellow-servants also and their brethren, who should be killed even as they were, should have fulfilled their *course.* (Revelation. 6:9-11)

Only in a human that loves God enough to endure suffering and death for God, does God have proof that Love's forgiveness can fully restore harmony between God and mankind. All other humans will be too busy worshipping the satisfaction of their desires and will not be able to suffer and die for God. Only those humans that know deeply that God loves and provides for them will ever be able to let go of the compulsive attempts at satisfying our human needs that is so destructive to humans.

If we are going to be able to endure this, our divine destiny (to suffer with Jesus, thus providing a faithful witness in God's courtroom), we will need, like our brethren before us, to get this revelation about Jesus. This revelation of Jesus is given, to those of us who are about to suffer, to prepare us for this suffering! That is its significance for us. Knowing that Jesus is what will restore everything to harmony again, and seeing it spelled out, in a big-picture form in this unveiling is what will give us the strength and courage to endure suffering for a time. The big picture in this unveiling is important; it is highly strengthening of our trust in Jesus.

Jesus suffered and is consequently shown to have been given all authority over sin and death and prideful rebellion. We too will suffer and we too will be given, as Jesus' administration, authority, and power over sin and death and rebellion. And in as much as we are given this power over the sin, death, and prideful rebellion within us, in the context of our walk of trust in Jesus, we also will bring God's judgment upon the sin, death, and prideful rebellion to the world around us.

By knowing just how much empowerment is awaiting us, we can thus endure the sacrificial suffering we are called to experience. As the writer of Hebrews said,

Looking unto Jesus the author and perfecter of our faith, ***who for the joy that was set before Him endured the cross***, despising shame, and hath sat down at the right hand of the throne of God. (Hebrews. 12:2).

This is an emotional, a psychological necessity. We cannot endure suffering without knowing that if we do we will be given divine authority and empowerment to rule with Jesus. This ruling with Jesus implies we will be returned to our natural Edenic state of functionality. Long has our species wondered if anything could bring actual change, bring real transformative healing to our human condition. This Unveiling of Jesus confirms for us that Jesus IS THAT CATALYST FOR CHANGE. It shows Jesus effectively judging what we are incapable of judging.

Those Christians that endure the suffering transformation Jesus leads us through will have seen God overcome compulsive behavior, and obsessive emotions in them. They will see Jesus change them from the selfish, fearful, people they were into a person that truly does love others, and often does so sacrificially.

I'm telling you, it will not simply be the coming of hard times that makes us able to change, as so many of us have assumed. Many souls will be destroyed by the coming hardship. It is by knowing that we will be empowered to rule (first our own dysfunctional humanity, and then the external world with Jesus), that we will be given what we emotionally need to endure. And endurance of the suffering coming to us from God brings change. We will need the truth of our eventual empowerment thoroughly spelled out (which is what the Revelation of Jesus does for us) for us to stand in that dark time.

And that dark time we will have to endure does not have to be the Tribulation Period at the end of the age. It can just be the hard periods of a typical human life, in which everything seems hopeless. And whatever kind of dark time we are given to endure, it will have the effect of transforming our life. God will make us able to trust Him.

Here is the way this trusting God thing works. We cannot trust God to resolve the *symptoms of* our disharmony with Him unless we are first rooted and grounded in faith/in trust in His Jesus-restoration of our status with God. No one cares about getting better if they are worried about being killed in the next moment. And no one cares about becoming more morally healthy if they are worried about God sending them to eternal damnation. We need to know Jesus made us acceptable to God before we can begin to think about trusting God to fix all that is immoral in us.

This Gospel, thus, needs to be spelled out to our hearts, not just our heads. Our heart has learned not to trust authority because of its long painful history of dysfunctional human tyranny and injustice. Our hearts cannot now simply choose to trust authority completely (even God's). It must be trained/conditioned by God to trust. First, we must come to trust that we are accepted in the beloved, even as He (Jesus) is. After choosing to accept loving forgiveness we can then begin to choose to follow Jesus' arch-example of trust as it relates to receiving healing/judgment of specific immoral areas of our human existence. And finally, even our physical needs will be something we can trust God for.

This choice, to trust in God in the painful transforming process, has been and will be for us followers of Jesus as difficult to endure as the Tribulation period will be for all mankind. It is the inner *tribulation all* believers in Jesus must endure. I hope you can understand and embrace this because this statement is not an exaggeration. The hardship we will experience will not simply arise from the discomfort of physical pain. It will be from the emotional and psychological pain that comes from our damaged idea of ourselves. This damaged idea of ourselves makes us run from suffering out of shame and fear of condemnation.

Thus, even our ability to endure God's restoration of our being will require that we get this revelation of Jesus. I cannot emphasize enough that the means God employs to restore our species to functionality is suffering and that that suffering will be terrible, for all of us. And that it will require Jesus, and all He represents in terms of God's complete forgiveness and the consequent acceptance of us, and His ability and intention to fully heal us, for us to be able to endure this transformative suffering.

So, the Revelation of Jesus is not primarily a book about the future; it is about Jesus' empowerment to take us through the healing process and restore harmony with God. Unless, and until, you get this you will never get the blessing stored up for us in this revelation, and worse yet, you may not get what you need to endure and shine in face of the trial that comes to His body first and is soon coming upon the whole earth.

(Revelation 1:4-8) John to the seven churches that are in Asia: Grace to you and peace, from him who is and who was and who is to come; and from the seven Spirits that are before his throne; and from Jesus Christ, who is the faithful witness, the firstborn of the dead, and the ruler of the kings of the earth. Unto him that loveth us, and loosed us from our sins by his blood; and he made us to be a kingdom, to be priests unto his God and Father; to him be the glory and the dominion for ever and ever. Amen. Behold, he cometh with the clouds; and every eye shall see him, and they that pierced him; and all the tribes of the earth shall mourn over him. Even so, Amen. I am the Alpha and the Omega, saith the Lord God, who is and who was and who is to come, the Almighty.

Note the 3-stage structure in the verse above. In highlighting this embedded structure one can see what is happening in the text more clearly.

Catalyst) Because John is a fellow partaker of the tribulation and governance and patience, which is the essence of a life in Jesus,

System) He was in a spiritual, divinely produced state of mind on God's day (the Sabbath/the time for rest/trust), and heard a great voice (important communication),

Outcome) that let him know that he should write down the things he would be shown,

and give them to the seven churches*(these seven churches fully define {7} the issues that represent the present community of followers of Jesus).*

As always, it is the effect of enduring the suffering (Catalyst) Jesus leads us through that makes us able to rest/trust (System), and this trust is what enables God to flow through us to the world around us (Outcome).

John, your fellow sufferer, within the context of God's governance, was separated by God.

As with the Apostle John, so with us, it is our suffering that sanctifies (separates) us to bring the revelatory and confirming word of God, and the testimony of Jesus, to you all.

Here again, the theme of suffering is raised to a highly important status.

Revelation 1:12-20 What It's All About

Revelation 1:12 And I turned to see the voice that spake with me.

Turning indicates a change in one's view of things. Seeing Jesus as the Priest of God, in all His glory, power, and authority, will require that we too undergo a change in perspective, from depending on self-righteous-legalism to trusting in the Lamb's blood. Since Adam's fall, there is not one person who will not need to have their mind changed about legalism. And unless we do, we cannot see Jesus judge our legalistic, self-righteous, rebellious self-rule-destroyed life. In other words, we are not able to see God as the source of what we need until He first convinces our hearts that we are not the source of what we need. Our King, Jesus will accomplish that by speaking to the issues in our hearts.

And having turned I saw seven golden candlesticks;

Having turned (having changed my point of view) I saw the High Priest keeping the lamp stands in the temple of God. This little detail in the description of events is not there for no reason. It holds meaning for us. Unless we have our view of legalism changed, we will not be able to truly see that Jesus is in charge of His Body. If we cannot rely on Jesus, to restore us to harmony (acceptability) with God, how can we possibly rely on Jesus to restore our dysfunctional being?

Why do I say that the turning/changing is about legalism? I say this because Adam and Eve's embrace of legalism is what the Bible specifies was the original turning *away from* God. **The fall of man rendered mankind legalistic. Legalism is now mankind's overwhelmingly dominant religious impulse. Contrary to what many Christians believe, it is not primarily a Jewish or a Christian problem. It is the religion of mankind since the fall, and it has simply not yet been erased completely from God's people.**

Revelation 1:13 and in the midst of the candlesticks one like unto a son of man, clothed with a garment down to the foot, and girt about at the breasts with a golden girdle.

Jesus, here depicted as our high priest, is attending the menorah in the temple. The clothes He is wearing are those of a temple priest. We are in this scenario described as being an instrument that conveys enlightenment on the subject of worship, of oneness with God (these lamps are in a temple). We are the lamp-stands/candlesticks/menorah. And it is Jesus' job to keep our light shining bright. This is another way of saying we do not perfect ourselves. It is Jesus who trims our wicks and fills our lamps. This opening description of Jesus, our high priest, in the temple of the Lord, is another key left by the front door of a section of text. It is summing up what is about to follow. Jesus will trim the wicks (purge/purify/discipline us) and thus empower us to enlighten the world around us about genuine trust in God, which is true worship. It will be God's love flowing through us that shows the world it can trust God.

And how does Jesus keep our lamps? He teaches us to trust God, by taking us through situations in which we *must* trust God (just as Jesus did His first disciples, and as God did to Israel in the wilderness). And He only does this if we follow Him wherever He leads us, into great vulnerability and adversity. Jesus is still disciplining us. We must not disciple ourselves. We have Jesus' spirit within us. We must follow where He leads us. This is a spiritual walk, not an intellectual, dogmatic walk. In fact, our intellect will consistently have a great deal of trouble understanding what God is doing in our lives, and will often be utilized by our pride to resist what God is doing in our life.

The Enlightenment We Are Meant To Embody For The Whole World Is The Truth Of What Human Life Looks Like When It Has Been Restored To Trusting Harmony With God.

Revelation 1:14 And his head and his hair were white as white wool, white as snow; and his eyes were as a flame of fire;

Jesus has a completely righteous relationship with authority (*white* is associated with righteousness/with harmony, and hair is associated with a covering/with authority.) and a purified perception of things (eyes of fire). Now, why do you suppose we need to know that Jesus has a harmonious relationship with authority and that His perception of things is pure? We need to know this because Jesus is about to judge us, His body, and judge the rest of God's creation as well.

If Jesus had issues with authority Himself, His judgments of us would be nothing more than Jesus seeing those problems in us that He could not face in Himself (i.e., He would be projecting on us His issues). His perspective is pure/is true. We also need to know He has the authority from God to judge us, and that when He does judge us His judgments will absolutely be a true representation of God's, of Love's perfect judgments.

Revelation 1:15 and his feet like unto burnished brass, as if it had been refined in a furnace; and his voice as the voice of many waters.

Jesus learned obedience by the things which He suffered (Heb. 5:8), and because He did, His walk (feet) is perfectly conformed to the will of God. Burnishing is a symbol of something made to shine via refining, via a more intimate, hands-on kind of judgment; with brass being the symbol of judgment. The manufacturing process known as burnishing is used to reshape something and change its finish (make it shine). Are you getting the picture here? Jesus, himself was burnished by God. He learned how to implement God's will/learned obedience by the things He suffered. And now He will lead us through this same kind of burnishing process. God will do the burnishing. He will, as the scriptures put it, transform us in the image of Jesus. The shining we will be capable of doing will manifest as us loving people the way God loves.

The things Jesus says are deeply resonant with us, like many waves (emotionally powerful). *{Water is symbolically associated with the soul, and* *specifically with that realm through which our emotions (symbolized as fish) indistinctly glide.}* The living word of God, Jesus is thus the only thing that truly resonates with and applies to our hearts.

The heart is our database of experiences and the lessons we have learned from them, good and bad, whether by fear's subjectivity or love's insight. And divine forgiveness is the most profoundly resonant experience of all.

Revelation 1:16 And he had in his right hand seven stars: and out of his mouth proceeded a sharp two-edged sword: and his countenance was as the sun shineth in his strength.

Our priest is conscious of and is in command of, the leaders of His flock (He has them in His right hand). He is speaking God's judgments to them (the sword of the spirit, the word of God). His personality *(His countenance is as the sun at noon)* is awe-inspiring and enlightening. Is this not true of the Jesus you have experienced? If it isn't, you have not yet personally experienced Jesus.

The number seven is associated with the full development of something. When a fetus is fully developed it is birthed and can then begin to live out its existence. The leaders of the flock of Jesus are the full development, the full expression, the full embodiment of Jesus. Even in our present state of dysfunction, we are already the embodiment of Jesus in that Jesus is showing His ability to govern the human condition in the stages of our development.

His countenance/His facial expression *(the face is associated with our personality and our state of mind expressing itself)* is that kind of personality and state of mind that reflects the truth (the light) of God, which is stated to be love. Jesus, the avatar of divine forgiveness, is the full expression of God's unconditional love. He/divine forgiveness is the fullest expression of it that there is in all of the universe. Think about it, can anything more fully express unconditional love than forgiveness by a perfect person of a very imperfect one?

Revelation 1:17 And when I saw him, I fell at his feet as one dead. And he laid his right hand upon me, saying, Fear not; I am the first and the last,

First, our cognitive understanding of what God wants to show us must be shut down (John is rendered unconscious). Then his spiritual understanding is awakened by God. In other words, like John, we need to be made conscious of something by being released from our human, purely intellectual view of it). From the vantage point of His position of authority, Jesus is about to state that He is God and that He has command of death, and Hades, the place of the dead. *{Death is a symbol of our dysfunction and Hades is a metaphor for our unresolved past, our unresolved memories of pain, from which all of our dysfunction comes.* Just as the dead await divine judgment in Hades, so too do our past unresolved experiences with pain await healing judgment by Love/by God. *Our bad behavior comes from our unresolved past experiences with pain. This is one of the most basic psychological realities about the human condition. PLEASE NOTICE THAT GOD KNOWS THIS PSYCHOLOGICAL REALITY.}*

Jesus is defined here as; the first, the last, and the living one. There is something profound being stated about Jesus here. He is both God (First and last), and the full manifestation of God in a living human form (the Living one). He is the avatar of divine forgiveness for our species.

On a technical note, referring to Jesus as the first and the last also implies that Jesus is the aspect of God that is expressed in time and space. This is consistent with the description of Him as the living eternal word of God. Jesus is what God has to say about everything. When the writer of Hebrews states…

Heb 1:2 Hath in these last days spoken unto us by his Son, whom he hath appointed heir of all things, by whom also he made the worlds;

Heb 1:3 Who being the brightness of his glory, and the express image of his person, and upholding all things by the word of his power, when he had by himself purged our sins, sat down on the right hand of the Majesty on high;

… he is saying Jesus is the aspect of God that effectively is everything in the material universe. If you hold everything together, then it would not exist without you. That means it *IS* you.

And this is the Jesus we are trusting when we believe He died for our sins and that divine forgiveness now governs with God the whole world's restoration process (including ours).

Anyone that works with the psychological issues of human beings knows that the dawning reality of forgiveness has the deepest, the most profound effect upon the damage done to the human being's idea of himself. And Jesus does not simply forgive our current sins, He also brings the healing work of forgiveness to our past sins, and to the past sins of others against us that have left us emotionally wounded. Jesus is thorough. He descended into the heart of man (Hades) and brought freedom to those parts of our humanity made a prisoner of our experiences with unresolved painful judgment and wounding.

Revelation 1:18 and the Living one; and I was dead, and behold, I am alive for evermore, and I have the keys of death and of Hades.

We need to become conscious of the truth that Jesus/that divine forgiveness is the beginning and completion of our restoration, and while He is on the topic of our restoration that He has the means to free (unlock with His keys/His insight) our unresolved memories of past wounding. Again, do you see God might have some understanding of how our psychological makeup works? He knows that He has to give us insight into what actually happened in our experiences with pain in order for them to be resolved. And Jesus will give us this insight into our experiences with pain if we follow Him into suffering.

Knowing that Jesus has authority over our hearts, and death and knowing Him to be the start and finish of all things, as well as being that which is eternal, is what makes it possible to see how God's unveiling of divine judgment will unfold. Otherwise, one's alienation from God will limit one's interest in the Unveiling to merely a prideful, destructive preoccupation with merely knowing future events.

Again let me say that because Hades is the place where dead souls await judgment, this marks it as being a reference to our unresolved memories of emotional wounding. Symbolically, the dead are those painful memories that still haunt our present, rendering us dysfunctional humans. Recall that it is said of Jesus that when He died he descended into Hades He took captivity captive. {Act 2; 27,31 and Psalm 16:-11, Ephesians 4:7-9}

Acts 2:25-28 - {New King James version} 25 For David says concerning Him: 'I foresaw the Lord always before my face, For He is at my right hand, that I may not be shaken. 26 Therefore my heart rejoiced, and my tongue was glad; Moreover my flesh also will rest in hope.

27 For You will not leave my soul in Hades, Nor will You allow Your Holy One to see corruption. 28 You have made known to me the ways of life; You will make me full of joy in Your presence.'

Ephesians 4:7-9

7 But unto every one of us is given grace according to the measure of the gift of Christ. 8 Therefore He saith, "When He ascended up on high, He led captivity captive, and gave gifts unto men."

9 (Now the saying, "He ascended" — what does it mean but that He also descended first into the lower parts of the earth? 10 He that descended is the same who also ascended up far above all heavens, that He might fill all things.)

Jesus' work in our life is anything but a superficial head trip.

As a person who has worked with the emotional damage in people's lives as a therapist, I would also like to point out here that divine forgiveness does need to be applied to both our failures and the failures of others, and this is as true about past experiences as it is about current ones. The way this looks in a healing process is that the patient must see that God has forgiven the failures of their relatives, in order for those aspects they inherit from them can be harmoniously used by God. Without this work of Jesus in our unresolved past, much of who we are will always look inherently evil to us, and so we will never be comfortable trusting God to use it.

Revelation 1:19 Write therefore the things which thou sawest, and the things which are, and the things which shall come to pass hereafter;

Knowing what God has to say about Jesus is to know the unfolding of future events. To attempt to know the future outside of the context of knowing Christ is to become confused and deluded about things. The entire history of the material universe is unfolding from Jesus, from God's gesture of forgiveness of beings designed to learn from experience.

Know Jesus in His Unveiling! Everything else will be able to be viewed in its actual context once you focus on knowing Jesus. The rest of the Bible becomes more clearly set within its context once you see Jesus in His Unveiling. This is a wonderful feature of the Unveiling of Jesus. It will make everything in the bible, everything in the universe, and everything in your own life more clearly understood. And that is an enormously comforting thing. *{I want to assert that I have not used exaggeration in anything I have said in this paragraph.}*

Revelation 1:20 the mystery of the seven stars, which thou sawest in my right hand, and the seven golden candlesticks. The seven stars are the angels of the seven churches: and the seven candlesticks are seven churches.

If you come to know Jesus, you will come to know Him as the High Priest and Judge of the Chosen. Jesus holds the seven stars in His right hand. This signifies Jesus holds the destiny, and consequently, the sanctification of His Body in His hands.

{Sanctification is a religious word that means to make something sacred. The Sanctification process thus implies that someone is taken through a process in which they are brought into harmony with God and can therefore be utilized by Him again. God can flow through this one again, thus enabling them to live a human life fully.}

The Body of Jesus, the community of Jesus' followers, is symbolically depicted as the menorah in the Temple of God. Without the menorah lighting up the temple, you would not see God or Jesus the High Priest. God has given us this high calling. We are the instruments God employs to show Himself and Jesus to the world.

If we only learn and pass on a bunch of religious doctrines to people, we remain in darkness and carry no enlightenment on the existence and the nature of Jesus and God to the world. We must have lives full of love for one another and the rest of the human species around us.

The truth of God is the light of God. **This light is only ever expressed as love.** God is stated to be love, and not merely to have love. **Truth May Be Defined As The Context Of Things**, which systematically unfolds itself in everything as an expression of love/of harmony. God is the context of things. This context of everything may only be understood by humans as we experience being loved. ***Love May Be Defined As The Embrace Of The Context, The Truth Of Things.***

Fear is the absence of this embrace of the context of things. In other words, it is disorientation. Fear damages our idea of ourselves/damages our identity. Feeling ourselves being loved reorients us. And love's forgiveness is what is needed to break through the natural resistance to receiving love in one that has suffered damage to their identity. This is how and why Jesus is given authority by God over all of His creation.

And we are to fully commit ourselves to follow Jesus, who is capable of governing the human condition/keeping the Menorah of God, rather than merely pursuing an intellectual grasp of moral or theological issues. Theology is meant to confirm our experience of God, not generate it. One must seek God, ask from God, and knock on God's door, so to speak. Without this questing to experience God, all the dogma in the world will remain just useless speculation, and worse, it will poison our relationships with people and kill our connection with God.

2Tim. 2:

14 Of these things put them in remembrance, charging them in the sight of the Lord, that they strive not about words, to no profit, to the subverting of them that hear.

15 Give diligence to present thyself approved unto God, a workman that needeth not to be ashamed, handling aright the word of truth.

16 But shun profane babblings: for they will proceed further in ungodliness,

17 and their word will eat as doth a gangrene:

Those who follow Jesus into suffering, and endure it until Jesus has rooted out of them all that is foreign to the rule of God, are this workman who need not be ashamed. To the extent that a person is unwilling to follow Jesus into suffering, and endure it until Jesus completes His work in them, to that extent they will need to make things about words (about theology, and arguments about theology/ideology). We who are the menorah of Jesus in God's temple **ARE** the theology that God means to use to communicate His will and nature to the world. We are the embodiment of Jesus on earth, Who is the living, eternal Word of God.

Those people, who won't follow Jesus into suffering, carry words that eat and kill like gangrene. This gangrene-like communication is another way of saying it is a mentality of condemnation rather than God's mentality of unconditional, forgiving love. The condemnation state of mind eats us up. It consumes us till we no longer are us.

These people are arrogant and selfish, hypocritical and condemning because only Jesus can give us any spiritual life. We can't give ourselves or others spiritual life. Without Jesus' work in our lives, we become spiritually hollow and full of insecurity and are just plain hypocrites. As Jesus said of the Pharisees in Matthew. 23, they will traverse earth and sea to find one convert, and when they have found him, make him twice the son of Hades as they are (they make them a product of their unresolved painful memories, or in other words, they make their converts as subjective as they are; no twice as much as they are. Such converts are enormously subjective and prone to project their un-faced issues onto everyone else).

Jesus is the one who holds our restoration in His hands. It is only by following Him that we become restored to sons and daughters of God. We don't hold our lives in our own hands. **We cannot arrogantly devise a plan for the restoration of our broken souls. Jesus must do this, and He will not share that plan with us, except in bits and pieces, as we need a little information just to continue following His leading.** After all, he does not want to encourage us to trust in our understanding (which is kind of a big problem with our species).

People who refuse to trust Jesus' lordship, and refuse to follow Him into healing suffering, are full of pride in their command of their life's restoration process.

They are full of agendas for themselves and everyone else. They compensate for the lack of real, or divine governance of their desires, emotions, and destiny by coercively grasping for control of everyone else's. Interestingly, the more a person disbelieves in God (whether they be religiously inclined or not), the less they believe in nature, and seek to work against it to survive.

Those who follow Jesus into suffering, and the death of pride and unbelief, and rebellion, are people who genuinely do not need to control you. Rather, because they actually trust God to be the thing that changes us they delight in validating and strengthening your freedom to do as you will. And to that end, these validators of the Will of others simply try to remain sensitive to whether or not their listeners wish them to tell what they see their options are.

Such followers of Jesus constantly see before their eyes Jesus in command of things. Their lives are a living confession that Jesus is Lord. They see Jesus in every event, in every situation, and in every seeming happenstance, and feel no need to do anything but let Jesus lead.

They see Jesus saving people from psychological issues and emotional wounding and horribly damaged identities, and so feel progressively less need to be saviors themselves. If they don't sense Jesus giving them any instruction or his leading as it relates to a problem or a need, they don't do anything. They will let a problem spin out of control before they take matters into their own hands.

And because of this real trust they have in Jesus' rule over their and other people's lives, people instantly know them to be people they can trust with their deepest needs and issues. No sensible person truly trusts those who are simply passionate teachers of theology. They may try to comply with them, but they don't ever trust them.

Rev. 2-3 The Application

In Jesus' address to the seven Ecclesias/churches, He refers to **Jezebel**, the **Nicolaitans**, and **Balaam**. All three are a symbol of, or the result of, self-righteousness. Self-righteousness is the religion we've turned to, trusted in, and followed since the fall. This is what these three evils look like in our church settings.

Jezebel: People that promote legalism to better dominate others via the skillful triggering of their wounded, condemning conscience.

Nicolaitans: Personality-cult leaders who seek to get other people to worship them by first triggering debilitating self-hatred in their followers (As though Jesus' sacrifice was not enough salvation), and then offering themselves as a spiritually superior human generously giving out salvation to all of us spiritually inferior losers.

Balaam: Treasonous leaders who sell out their fellow followers of Jesus for financial security. It is typical in Christian communities to be a person spouting some new-fangled version of the knowledge of good and evil. The alternative to this is to tear down that alter to self-worship and promote total trust in God for the transformation of the human condition. The

Balaam in our midst will seek to pander to the popular tastes of those that pay their salary. They will not risk the loss of their salary by preaching trust in God's ability to govern the human condition by His spirit. So, in order to remain secure in their job they will promote the teaching of self-righteous legalism by other teachers even though they themselves do not hold with such lies. This is such a widespread problem in Christian communities that I am confident no one will have the least difficulty understanding what I am referring to in this Balaam issue.

In the following pages of this book, we will be looking into the meaning of these three evil factors. Together, they represent the ways that mankind has chosen to trust in his human resources to govern his dysfunctional soul.

As you read through these addresses of Jesus to the seven churches, know that you are all seven of these churches, not just the good ones. Say to God, I am the church of Ephesus; I am the church of Smyrna; I am the church of Pergamum; I am the church of Thyatira; I am the church of Sardis; I am the church of Philadelphia, and I am the church of Laodicea. Judge/heal me, Jesus.

Doing this may make you wince when you come to some of the less savory churches, or blush with skepticism when you come to the more wonderful churches, but the truth is, if you are following Jesus, you ARE each of these churches, good and awful. Jesus gave us these addresses because He is our Lord. He intends that we know that He can and will perfect our trust in God if we follow Him wherever He leads, with no stipulations, holding nothing back. You won't have to see all of these issues immediately, but eventually, Jesus will bring each up in your life.

The seven churches constitute all of the most fundamental issues that need judging in us to be able to follow Jesus into suffering. This is how we will become transformed into the likeness of Jesus. Thus, we must come to be convicted by God's spirit of these issues. Don't run from the Sardis and Laodicea in you. Ask God to show you where those churches are in you. I promise you, they are there.

In this section Jesus, as our High Priest, tends His menorah in God's temple. Note the structure of each of these seven judgments. First, there is the opening statement in which Jesus says something about Himself that will be relevant to that Church. Secondly, the judgment will be based upon the standard of perfection just revealed in Jesus' character. He then concludes with a statement in which He offers a promise to that church. Every one of these seven judgments follows this format.

This entire JESUS JUDGING THE CHURCHES section is also divided into three subsections. The first section is spoken to Ephesus and, as with every first section; one can see that it is the key to unlocking the meaning of the whole message. The second section is spoken to Smyrna, Pergamum, and Thyatira, in support of this opening point. The third section is spoken to Sardis, Laodicea, and Philadelphia, bringing those points to their conclusion.

Catalyst -Ephesus Rev. 2:1-7

The Main Thing I Need To Judge In The Church Is That You Have Left Your First Love

Revelation 2:1 To the angel of the church in Ephesus write: These things saith he that holdeth the seven stars in his right hand, he that walketh in the midst of the seven golden candlesticks:

I authorize the leaders of the church (*I hold the seven stars in My hand*). In other words, Jesus is saying; I'm whom you must account to. This implies that they were more concerned about man's opinion of them than God's. It is only because we are more concerned about man's opinion of us that we come to leave our first love. Jesus is about to charge them with not knowing who their boss is. The fact these seven stars are held in Jesus' right hand symbolizes that Jesus is conscious of and is overseeing your state of enlightenment, your spiritual condition. The right symbolizes consciousness, the left symbolizes unconsciousness.

Stars are a metaphor for divinely given examples of enlightenment meant to be followed. God means to enlighten the Christian community through the example given by the leaders in Jesus' Church. This implies that Jesus must judge not only His church but the leaders. They must become examples of the enlightened trusting human existence God wants us all to be. In the same way that God must judge His church before judging the world, so too must He judge the leaders before judging the rest of Jesus' body.

Defining the leaders as an example of enlightened human existence also means that the issues of the leaders of Jesus' Body are inextricably interwoven with the issues of their congregation. We cannot afford to see ourselves as separate from each other. Leaders cannot complain about their followers' condition, and their congregants cannot complain about the condition of the leaders. We must see that we have those issues that we see in each other.

Leaders that have not been authorized by God, but instead were chosen only by man, will not allow themselves to be brought under Jesus' oversight and judgment. Anyone can see the difference between these two kinds of leadership. Man-chosen leadership caters to men. Jesus-chosen leadership caters to Jesus, even at the expense of their connection with men.

{Of course, even Jesus' chosen leaders cater to men somewhat, in as much as the gospel has not yet been thoroughly embraced by any man. We are all in the process of embracing it more and more deeply. Yet the leadership choices and actions that come from Jesus cater to Him, and not men.}

Stating that Jesus holds church leaders in His right hand is necessary because, strangely enough, many leaders think they must account to man. They are man-pleasers. Let me describe how that comes to be.

When the wonder of God's gift of forgiveness and acceptance fades, it becomes replaced in our thoughts with a fear-driven focus on the state of our soul's restoration. This fixation with our moral state renders us focused on man's opinion of us because we no longer feel comfortable hearing God's opinion of us. **A change of focus from our relationship with God to our moral condition always manifests as self-righteous, legalistic hypocrisy**.

The fear of man replaces our fear of God. Fear, used in this sense, is defined as respectful accountability to the one you are dependent upon. Whomever you are dependent upon you respect and become accountable to. We can't depend on God to forgive us, and then trust our restoration to the religious people we are hanging around with. If we do we will depend upon humans, and by extension, human strength to take our dysfunctional souls through restoration.

False accountability tends to become institutionalized in the form of the roles we give our leaders. We make our leaders mediators between God and us, and we do this because we don't yet know that we already have an effective mediator with God in Jesus. Somehow, in our minds, they become inherently spiritually superior to us.

In the body of Jesus, we are not meant to account to men for our state of restoration. There currently exists an evil doctrine that has become popular among many Christian communities. It is overtly stated that we should be in *accountability relationships with* other people. Yet, we will only ever account to whom we depend upon to judge us. He who judges us must take us through the restoration process. That is Jesus alone. We may submit to/that is, support each other, as we would God, (for it is Jesus/God in them we are supporting) but we must account only to God. Sneaky little deception, this.

In this verse, Jesus, by saying He holds the leaders of His followers in His hands, is correcting what has long been a problem among His followers; they have forgotten to whom they must account; they have lost sight of who will shepherd them through the restoration process and so they lead the rest of us into self-governance. We have become legalistic hypocrites who preach sermons on what **we have to do to** access what Jesus provided for us by His death on the cross. If we need to do anything other than follow Jesus' leading in our dysfunctional lives, then what Jesus accomplished by His death and resurrection is empty of power to change us.

This accountability to man instead of to He who holds our candlesticks is an immense problem in Christian communities. Like leaven that saturates a lump of dough, this spiritual leaven has saturated the Christian community. It is a form of what Jesus referred to as the leaven of the Pharisees.

Yes, because we have come to depend upon and account to men for our soul's restoration, we also have come to depend upon men to take the collective soul of our Christian community through the restoration process. When this misplaced trust in man proves less than effective at solving all of our community's problems or meeting all of our community's needs, we typically resort to our human resources to address this failure in church leaders. And our human resources look like us destructively complaining and slandering or as the many forms of back-room scheming and power-politics that spring up in our Christian communities. Thus we have become hypocritical, legalistic, bitter, divisive, spiritually lifeless, non-committal people.

If we continue to follow Jesus who has saved our souls from disharmony with God, we will be led into all kinds of restoration, and this will encourage us to trust God with the restoration of our fellow believers. This, in turn, will inevitably unify us with our fellow followers, in as much as we are not disturbing one another by our attempts at restoring anything, either within ourselves or in others. And when we are unified, God will bless us with a move of His spirit.

Revelation 2:2 I know thy works, and thy toil and patience, and that thou canst not bear evil men, and didst try them that call themselves apostles, and they are not, and didst find them false;

I know you work hard for the kingdom of God, and I see your patience and that you won't tolerate evil men who say they are apostles/emissaries sent from Me, but aren't. Clearly, a person can work hard, and with patience, and can have the integrity to not tolerate evil men, and yet have lost that first love for and accountability to God.

But Jesus liked that they tried those that named themselves emissaries/apostles of God but weren't, and found them false. This showed that they still had some genuine trust in Jesus. A false emissary will ALWAYS need you to trust them to get you the spiritual goods. They will pose as a middle-man between God (or whatever ideal thing you are desiring) and you. So, if you are trusting Jesus, their attempts to get you to change who you trust will be greatly offensive to you.

Jesus hates those false apostles because they pose as mediators between God and man. Jesus alone is the source of all we need from God. There are a lot of these people running around today in Jesus' flock. Many of them have impressive television or internet ministries. Steer clear of them.

Revelation 2:3 and thou hast patience and didst bear for my name's sake, and hast not grown weary.

I know you've been patient, and suffered for My name's sake. And you don't let yourself get tired of doing all this.

I find myself responding; *Okay, I mean really! What more do you expect from these folks, Jesus? These people sound amazing. How many Christian communities do you know that are half this good?*

These people don't grow weary and are long-suffering for Jesus because they refuse to put their trust in men. They put it in God. Yes, they do trust in God for their righteousness and their physical and material needs, but they answer to their conscience, their understanding of things, and rely upon their human strength/their willpower for the transformation they need. This has caused them to leave their first love (of Jesus) and turn their attention to (and have affection for) man's opinion of them.

Revelation 2:4 But I have this against thee, that thou didst leave thy first love.

Here's Jesus' answer. But, the love is gone. You have forgotten the love you had when you first felt the grace of God's total forgiveness of you. That is this first *love Jesus* is referring to. Humans function better when they feel loved, and no one feels more loved than that moment they first trusted God to forgive them. And we lose this awareness of God's love for us because we begin to focus on our moral condition. We may well still be trusting God for that ultimate eternal acceptance of us (we are going to heaven), but we have stopped relishing the continued support that continued forgiveness offers us. Jesus is telling us all right here; that is a bad move.

When we make this wrong turn, away from a fixation on Jesus being our ongoing righteousness with God, we tend to not only focus on our moral condition but also tend to place our trust in our understanding of the bible. ***Intellectually Knowing biblical theology has never transformed anyone.*** *One must FEEL loved!* I emphasize the word *feel* because it is the emotional feeling of being loved that is the factor that brings the change in us. Our feeling loved is the precise thing that motivates us powerfully to create, account for our behavior, be productive, change course when needed, and sacrifice for the well-being of others. And Jesus is God's way of making sure we feel loved. If we don't feel loved, we are not loving others or ourselves. If we don't feel loved, it is because we are not following and trusting in Jesus to not only save us from eternal damnation but also to transform us. The high value we place on man's approval of us is the manifestation of our distrust in Jesus' ability to change us. And Jesus knows this is so.

Revelation 2:5 Remember therefore whence thou art fallen, and repent and do the first works; or else I come to thee, and will move thy candlestick out of its place, except thou repent.

If you don't change that and fixate once again upon *My* forgiveness of you, I will leave. The works you did when it was all about My grace to you, and love for you, are no longer happening. Now you increasingly do only what you feel conscience-bound to do. It's not the same!

Jesus says He will *remove their candlestick out of its place* if they don't repent and do those deeds that are generated by their first love. What does He mean by this statement? A candlestick, or lampstand as it once was long ago, is a device used to bring light to a particular area. The communities of followers of Jesus are meant to exist, not for the pleasure and convenience of ourselves, but in support of the strategic plans of Jesus. Jesus places communities of His followers in their locations to light up that location with the light of God's love. Jesus is God's lighting expert. If we don't make our relationship with God about His sacrificial forgiving love for us, and our natural response to that love, if we make our relationship with Him about our Christian duty, Jesus will leave. He will dramatically leave so that no one will ever confuse the kind of dogma-driven, obligation-driven community you have become with a community of His true followers.

If people see you as being more about correct theology than love, then you are not lighting up the location God has placed you in. And if you are not feeling God's love, you are not giving His love, His light, to others. In the Gospel of John, Jesus said...

John 15:

1 I am the true vine, and my Father is the husbandman.

2 Every branch in me that beareth not fruit, he taketh it away: and every *Branch* that beareth fruit, he cleanseth it, that it may bear more fruit.

3 Already ye are clean because of the word which I have spoken unto you.

4 Abide in me, and I in you. As the branch cannot bear fruit of itself, except it abide in the vine; so neither can ye, except ye abide in me.

5 I am the vine, ye are the branches: He that abideth in me, and I in him, the same beareth much fruit: for apart from me ye can do nothing.

6 If a man abide not in me, he is cast forth as a branch, and is withered; and they gather them, and cast them into the fire, and they are burned.

7 If ye abide in me, and my words abide in you, ask whatsoever ye will, and it shall be done unto you.

8 Herein is my Father glorified, that ye bear much fruit; and *so* shall ye be my disciples.

9 Even as the Father hath loved me, I also have loved you: abide ye in my love.

10 If ye keep my commandments, ye shall abide in my love; even as I have kept my Father's commandments, and abide in his love.

11 These things have I spoken unto you, that my joy may be in you, and *that* your joy may be made full.

12 This is my commandment, that ye love one another, even as I have loved you.

13 Greater love hath no man than this, that a man lay down his life for his friends.

14 Ye are my friends, if ye do the things which I command you.

15 No longer do I call you servants; for the servant knoweth not what his lord doeth: but I have called you friends; for all things that I heard from my Father, I have made known unto you.

16 Ye did not choose me, but I chose you, and appointed you, that ye should go and bear fruit, and *that* your fruit should abide: that whatsoever ye shall ask of the Father in my name, he may give it you.

17 These things I command you, that ye may love one another.

In Jesus' preaching, we see the equation of Jesus holding and judging the lampstands.

1. We will account to God.

2. We cannot bear fruit unless we abide in Jesus.

3. Abiding in Jesus is abiding in His love's forgiveness of us.

4. If we abide in Jesus, He will cleanse us.

5. If we abide in Jesus, and He cleanses us, the work we do will be to love others as He has loved us.

6. Jesus commanded us to love. If we abide in Him, we will do as He commanded, because He will cleanse us. This is the fruit Jesus is looking for in us.

7. If we don't bear fruit, it is because we don't abide in Jesus, and if we don't abide in Jesus, we will be cast into the fire (we will go through purging). Those that reject Jesus altogether will undergo eternal purging in the proverbial lake of fire. Those that have received Jesus as their righteousness with God, yet do not make their entire life about Jesus' gift of righteousness, Jesus will lead those into the purging of their self-righteousness by suffering. All of us followers of Jesus have some of this Ephesian kind of church in us, and it will require Jesus to purge us. But this means that He will not forsake us. He will do what needs to be done in us to make us able to trust in God completely.

Even this harsh judgment from Jesus is an incredible expression of mercy and faithful love. We humans are in terrible shape and yet Jesus is wholly committed to our restoration.

If we construct much of our life, our abode, based/founded upon deeds generated by our human strength, *God will discard us from being a part of Jesus' church/lampstand.* We will make it into heaven, but God will distance Himself from our life. He will not be associated with us in the minds of onlookers. We must construct our entire life upon the acceptance we have with God by Jesus' sacrifice for our sins.

Just because you call yourself a Christian, or say you have been saved, or born again, etc. does not mean you are abiding in Jesus. Etymologically, *abiding in* means to *remain in a given place.* Where are you at? Our own house is where we are consciously at in life, and so is a symbol for our thought life. We must build our entire life on Jesus taking away our sins (by His death on the cross) and making us acceptable to God.

Why would anyone who calls themselves a Christian build a life for themselves upon anything other than Jesus? Well, we humans will do that if:

~ we think we will be judged in comparison to other people, and feel that we compare favorably.

~ we think that the only ones we have to impress or be accepted by are our fellow men, not God.

If we want a relationship with God, we will not hold to either of these fallacies. They only exist to enable us to remain in a state of denial about our true dysfunctional state, and our true lack of harmony with God. So, if we truly do want a relationship with God we will face our need for a Savior and be desirous of building our whole life upon His forgiveness of us. And if we do build our life upon His forgiveness, we will have put ourselves into His hands, trusting Him to lead and provide, transform and protect us.

Whoever we trust to save us (and then to restore/cleanse us) is who we yield control of our life to. In this place of dependence upon Jesus we will submit to His cleansing of our souls. The soap He will use in our cleansing will be suffering and the water will be His personally communicated word to us. His words personally spoken to us become the joy that is set before us (His promise of transformation and the resulting empowerment to serve God), for which we endure the cleansing/cross. This word also manifests as the encouragement, insight, and strength we need to continue trusting Him to change us.

*Hebrews. 12:2 **looking unto Jesus** the author and perfecter of our faith, who for the joy that was set before him endured the cross, despising shame, and hath sat down at the right hand of the throne of God.*

Revelation 2:6 But this thou hast, that thou hatest the works of the Nicolaitans, which I also hate.

Jesus tells us, but one thing you do that truly pleases Me is you hate the actions of those personality cult leaders who try to set themselves up as mediators between God and men. These are those who I was referring to as people who call themselves apostles but are not.

The thing I hate about them is not just that they claim authority that I have not given them, but that they are acting as mediators between God and you. I, Jesus, am the only mediator between God and you. Following them effectively cuts people off from Me and God. It is not possible to trust your salvation or restoration to them and Me both.

{Personality cult figures are those people that are so filled with self-loathing (as a result of childhood traumas that left them feeling valueless) that they crave the worship of people. And in setting themselves up as a human that is somehow inherently superior to other humans (and thus worthy of being followed) they invariably will presume to take the place of Jesus as the savior and restorer of mankind.}

Revelation 2:7 He that hath an ear, let him hear what the Spirit saith to the churches. To him that overcometh, to him will I give to eat of the tree of life, which is in the Paradise of God.

If you conquer this problem of your fear of man, I will feed you from the tree that produces life. This tree is what we currently refer to as the autonomous unconscious. It is what the bible refers to as the *spirit-man* within or the human spirit. When our species fell out of harmony with God we likewise lost harmony with our spiritual self. This spiritual aspect of us is a part of God, who is spirit. God, and the human spirit, cannot sin. The autonomous unconscious mind of our species is pure objectivity/ it sees everything in its context. Our civilized view of it as being a cauldron of suppressed emotions and desires is based on a simple misunderstanding. Our cognitive mind frequently becomes threatened (and thus, more subjective) when the contents of the unconscious mind emerge into cognitive awareness. This does not mean that those contents are subjective. It is our cognitive mind that finds it difficult to process those contents. Our unconscious mind is supremely objective.

In trying to understand why such, often disturbing, and/or morally reprehensible contents would emerge from our unconscious mind, we leaped to the conclusion that our unconscious mind is just a storehouse of the suppressed contents our cognitive mind could not find a useful place for. The truth though is that those contents are all loaded with metaphorical meaning. What appear to be morally reprehensible thoughts emerging from the unconscious mind are instead symbolically encoded messages to our relatively subjective and task-oriented cognitive minds.

And those messages have almost entirely gone, ever since the fall of man, without being effectively received. Humankind is precisely as afraid of His unconscious mind as he is of god. Study the wealth of religious ideas formulated about the gods/goddesses throughout human history. You can easily see that we attribute to the gods the very same seeming misbehavior we have thought our unconscious mind was stirring up in us via its morally reprehensible emergent content. Gods of immense violence and catastrophe, and obsession and compulsive behaviors are behaving the same way we perceive the human unconscious mind behaving.

Of course we humans do not only fear the unconscious mind. We also are powerfully drawn to it, just as we are to God. Observe the more pleasing contents emerging whole from the unconscious mind of man. There is creativity, insight, intuition, the instinctual forces that carry us through life, and there is love. So, we have this strange love-dread, relationship with our unconscious mind, and it has led to us both suppressing the daylights out of it and to trying to control it (via magical formulas). Neither suppression of it nor our feeble attempts at exploiting it are expressions of us being in harmony with it. Only by us walking out our life in harmony with God (in Jesus) can we once again productively feed on this tree of life.

This feeding on the tree of life manifests as us seeing the object-lessons Jesus is teaching us. An example of an object lesson is the story of Jesus taking the disciples out on the sea of Galilee and then promptly falling asleep when a storm whips up and threatens to drown them all. Jesus awakens and then tells the storm to stop. It does stop, and they learn the lesson that Jesus is bigger than the storms we encounter in life.

Metaphorical meaning is not generated by our cognitive mind. It emerges whole from our objective unconscious mind. And in this example, you can see the purpose God has in forming this aspect of our being. It is there to give us objectivity and liberation from our fears. There are a host of other ways the tree of life communicates with our cognitive mind, and we humans have lost our ability to understand those forms. Every impulse, every mentality, every attitude, and every emotion emerging from the unconscious mind contains an encoded message for us, and only a harmonious connection with God in Jesus will unlock this resource.

It is because we do not understand what our spirit is saying to our cognitive mind in these emergent contents that we come to destructively, blindly follow those contents in a literal way, without decoding the symbolism. For example, we have an impulse to commit adultery. Surely, we think, God does not want us to have such an impulse. Yet the purpose of such impulses is that they are God's way of saying that we are *already* under the power of spiritual adultery. We are being unfaithful to our real selves.

The scariness, the disturbing nature of such a destructive impulse is also useful in that it is God's way of getting our attention. We are not wanting to face our inner adultery. We civilized humans are being untrue to ourselves in so many ways, so God has our unconscious minds give us this little disturbing pageant loaded with metaphorical meaning to reveal it to us. Again, it is because we are not in harmony with God that we fail to get these messages, and thus come to live out these very destructive impulses, compulsions, obsessions, etc.

These communiqués from our unconscious mind are God speaking to us. They are flowing constantly. All cognitive thought is constructed from the associations stored in our unconscious mind. It is kind of funny that we humans so often complain that God does not speak to us. He is talking to all of us non-stop. We just require the healing effect of divine forgiveness to be comfortable listening to Him.

If you think I am just making all this stuff concerning the unconscious mind up, note the part of the Eden story in which God posts angels to keep humans out of the garden and away from the tree of life. This little detail in the story of mankind's fall from its natural and functional existence is all about the damaged relationship we have with our unconscious mind. It is this loss of the consistent flow of objectivity from our tree of life, from our autonomous unconscious mind, that is responsible for our species' manifest cluelessness about its issues. Can you now begin to see just how much we lost in the fall of Adam and Eve? We are a shell of our former selves. We are limping toward self-destruction, ravaged by the subjectivity of our cognitive mind's pride and fears. AND JESUS/DIVINE FORGIVENESS IS THE CURE FOR THIS PROBLEM.

And in this address to the Ephesian church, Jesus is telling them, I will restore a viable harmonious connection with your unconscious mind if you will conquer this change-of-focus issue. This overcoming will manifest as you pursue your relationship with God before the improvement of your performance. If you don't put your relationship with God before the improvement of your performance, Jesus says He will remove your right to be counted among His lampstands.

This catalyst section of Jesus' address to his church is the idea that we need to put our relationship with God before our relationship with our moral growth/healing (manifested by us fixating not on our moral growth but focussing on our forgiveness in Jesus' sacrifice). Making this concept the catalyst section implies that all that comes after it will in some way embody this very issue.

SYSTEM - Smyrna Pergamum, Thyatira Rev. 2:8-11

This second section comprises Smyrna, Pergamum, and Thyatira. This second section comprises Smyrna, Pergamum, and Thyatira. It is saying that only Jesus can resurrect our deceased spiritual life (Smyrna), and that if you embrace my judgment it will transform you (Pergamum), and that you are about to have your perceptions and your walk judged by Me, Jesus (Thyatira).

Smyrna

Revelation 2:8 And to the angel of the church in Smyrna write: These things saith the first and the last, who was dead, and lived again:

I am The origin and the completion. I died and was resurrected. You need to hear this from Me, because you have chosen to put your trust in Me to finish what I started in you, and you are now being opposed in your trust in me. This opposition is both within you, in terms of the dying self-righteous mind that remains in you, and in the persecution from those around you who are arrogantly, self-righteously attempting to originate their own transformation. Everything that will be addressed in this message will be about this issue regarding the perfecting of your trust/faith.

Revelation 2:9 I know thy tribulation, and thy poverty (but thou art rich), and the blasphemy of them that say they are Jews, and they art not, but are a synagogue of Satan.

I know about your great hardships, and your material and social poverty (but you're really very rich). I know about those who are saying they are My people, but aren't, and that they slander you, saying that you are spiritual failures because you are not as financially successful and as socially empowered, as they. They are instead a community of spiritually rebellious pride (a synagogue/church of Satan).

Revelation 2:10 Fear not the things which thou art about to suffer: behold, the devil is about to cast some of you into prison, that ye may be tried; and ye shall have tribulation ten days. Be thou faithful unto death, and I will give thee the crown of life.

The suffering of the Church at Smyrna was literal. They were persecuted by those in leadership positions in their apostate religious community. For the Christians of that day, the religious community of Jewish people in the city of Smyrna was not as distinct from them as Jews and Christians are today. Many of the Christians in Smyrna likely came from and grew up in that Jewish community. For that Jewish community to think of themselves as a community of God-worshippers, and then to persecute the followers of Jesus was something many Jewish followers of Jesus in Smyrna had to live with and endure.

The analog of that situation today would not be Jewish people, but the religious people in the Christian church we have grown up in that do not truly follow Jesus. These people will think of themselves as a church of God/Christ, but Jesus wants us to know that He judges them as being a church of pride. Satan is the metaphor, par-excellence of pride. Being a church/synagogue of Satan in our day is being a community of Christians that cling to their pride, and persecute those that follow Jesus wherever He leads them. You may think of yourself as righteous or as Christian, and yet do not follow Jesus. When you run into those that do, you will (just like the Jewish people that would not truly trust in Jesus's saving work that existed in John's day), have a powerful impulse to persecute them. Their freedom to follow Jesus will stand as an obnoxious example of genuine righteousness/genuine harmony with God, convicting you of your unrighteous state.

These apostate leaders are not ever addressed by Jesus in The Revelation of Jesus. He ignores them and speaks only to those in the community that follows Him. The only reference Jesus makes to those apostate people comes when He refers to them as being Satan's church (not His). This is because they aren't Jesus' church.

This situation is one that most if not all we who follow Jesus will be called to experience at some point or another. We will find ourselves in a minority position, a position of being marginalized, rejected, or even oppressed by those in the mainstream of our religious community. And it will be because we are following Jesus that this rejection and persecution is happening to us.

Jesus knows that there are parts of all believers that are apostate (have fallen away from trusting in Jesus to redeem and consecrate us.). The apostasy of those in positions of power within our community is a mirror of those aspects of our hearts that have stopped trusting in Jesus. As we endure the suffering that comes from persecution by those external apostates, the internal distrust still present in us gets resolved by Jesus. It is thus the perfect means of resolving such internal disbelief, and our Savior and King knows this.

The crown we will receive if we endure this suffering *(we are not asked to do anything else by Jesus)*, is a metaphor for His authorizing us to rule and providing the empowerment necessary to do so. In these religious communities, we are painfully powerless and marginalized. Jesus is promising to give us God's power to govern and the social position this implies. This empowerment may or may not take place in this life, yet it absolutely will take place. Ideally, such empowerment is enjoyed in an age ruled by Jesus. It can only ever be temporary in this one.

The apostate leaders are people who have lives that look successful and are socially celebrated and empowered, but their success and social empowerment are superficial. They are like the rich man in the *Lazarus and the rich man* parable. They will get to have their social prosperity now. Later on, they will have to suffer. We who follow Jesus will experience suffering now, and suffer from living socially condemned lives, but later we will get to have great prosperity and great social authority.

If Your Empowerment (Social Or Economic) Did Not Come From The Suffering That God Has Led You Through, It Is Not From God, It Is From Men, And Will And Must Pass Away.

The suffering we undergo at the hands of the superficially empowered and superficially thriving mainstream part of our religious community forces us (that part of us that still wonders if we should be the source of our empowerment and thriving) to face our distrust in God and to die to pride within us. We look at their seeming success, and then look at our lamentable circumstance, and wonder if perhaps they are doing things right. And the process of enduring suffering cleanses us of all our distrust in God's absolute power to *raise up and set down kings*. King David experienced this very sort of dying, and ended up gloriously empowered and singing, "*My Glory and the lifter of my head*".

{Rev. 2:10 Fear not the things which thou art about to suffer: behold, the devil is about to cast some of you into prison, that ye may be tried; and ye shall have tribulation ten days. Be thou faithful unto death, and I will give thee the crown of life.}

The number ten is the symbolic expression of that which is complete, whole. *{Recall Jesus' use of ten virgins, ten coins, and 100 sheep. All multiples of ten are expressions of wholeness and the painful process we must endure to regain lost wholeness. This restoration process must be complete/be whole for it to effectively make **us** complete.}* Unwholeness is essentially all of the unnatural, dysfunctional, compulsive, suppressed, fear-driven behavior in us that has resulted from our inability to trust God for all that we need. When we can't trust God, we compensate by trusting ourselves to come up with what we need, and we can't come up with what we need so we strive and we fake it. Unwholeness is artificial human existence (it is not made by God), and worse, it generates all of the hurtful things we do to each other and ourselves because our life is so artificially and ineffectually put together by us.

We are broken humans, and Jesus means to fix us. He will do this by perfecting our trust in Him, via the tribulation we are taken through. In this time of trial, we learn who is truly God (our source of life), and who isn't. We learn who should have our trust, and who shouldn't. We learn this in a time of trial because in that place of hardship, faking it is no longer an option for us. We need real help with our life issues. Artificial help won't cut it.

Revelation 2:11 He that hath an ear, let him hear what the Spirit saith to the churches. He that overcometh shall not be hurt of the second death.

If you want to hear what God has to say to you, then listen to what His Spirit is saying to the ecclesia. Listen to Me about this and you won't suffer when God judges everyone at the Judgment of the world (Because you will already have faced His judgment). I mean to judge you now. Submit to the hard things I am about to say to you and you won't have to hear these things when I say them in My judgment on the whole world. That's your option here. Be judged now, and be empowered, or be judged when I judge the whole world and be destroyed. Or, in other words,**if you embrace my judgment it will transform you. But if you reject it, it will consume/will destroy you.** I hope you hear this, those of you who are reading this. This is for you and me. It is not for that reprobate Christian out there. And the time to heed this warning is now.

Pergamum Rev. 2:12-17

Revelation 2:12 and to the angel of the church in Pergamum write: These things saith he that hath the sharp two-edged sword:

What I am about to say to you is based upon the truth that I'm whom you have to account to. I am your judge/I have the sword. I need to tell you this because you are so concerned about how man sees you that you don't even know that I intend to judge you. You fear what man thinks of you and don't know that you should be concerned about what I think of you.

Revelation 2:13 I know where thou dwellest, even where Satan's throne is; and thou holdest fast my name, and didst not deny my faith, even in the days of Antipas my witness, my faithful one, who was killed among you, where Satan dwelleth.

I know it isn't easy being My follower in the capital city of prideful rebellion (Satan is the symbol for prideful rebellion, and Pergamum was filled with the fervent fertility cult kind of self-righteousness that is the essence of rebellion against God).

And you have retained your trust in Me even after you had to pay a dear price for this. They lived in a society that was antagonistic toward any kind of trust in God and had to pay a high price for their faith.

Pergamum's fertility cult worship drew upon a self-righteous, codependent earning of God's favor. Antipas was killed because he would not repent of his rejection of and opposition to their self-righteous gods. Self-righteousness is militant and murderous. This militancy goes all the way back to Cain in our species. Pagan gods are a personification of mankind's trust in human strength and deeds to generate the life we need.

At his trial, Antipas was commanded to worship the Roman emperor, knowing that a follower of Jesus would not do so, and knowing that refusal to worship the Roman emperor would be cause for his execution. He was executed by being roasted to death inside the bronze bull that sat atop the altar to Zeus.

Now, how many of us could choose this Antipas-like outcome today? Can you see that trust in our human strength would never afford us the strength to make such a choice? Only the power of God's spirit, made by His therapeutic work in our hearts, could generate such a decision in us. Human willpower can't overcome the terror that facing such an outcome would stir in us. Antipas was given what he needed to make this choice by God.

These and the rest of the literal facts associated with the Church of Pergamum are being used metaphorically to make a point. We can hold fast to Jesus' name, that is, that Jesus is Lord and Savior, and yet still engage in fertility cult worship (which is a symbol for legalism, the veneration of life above the one that creates life). Jesus is NOT simply railing against literal fornication, but against what the fertility cult practices symbolically represented, spiritual fornication *(which was metaphorically represented in the practice common at that place and time, of the ritual intercourse with prostitutes, who were seen as the embodiment of the Goddess)*. To think this passage is to be taken only literally is to render it obsolete for contemporary Christians, in as much as this kind of *Heiros Gamos (sacred prostitution)* fertility cult ritual is seldom practiced in human societies today.

Even so, the ideas behind these pagan fertility practices were (and are still) deeply ingrained in the peoples of the world. For example, there was still fertility cult worship of the gods and goddesses, barely disguised as the veneration of Christian saints, up until the 18th century in Europe. One would, within the local church, rub the saint's head, or even more obviously, make contact with, in some way, a phallus (penis object) or Yoni (vagina object) covertly placed in the church to ensure that one would get pregnant. This is a classic example of fertility cult worship.

A person wanted to ensure that they had some production of life (such as pregnancy or good crops) and thus worshipped this longed-for life in its iconic form. In the same way that Pagan fertility veneration has proved amazingly persistent in human culture, in the same way, legalism is deeply engrained within the human psyche and by extension, within human culture. And yes, Jesus does not want us to engage in these literal cult practices, but it is what they represented, legalistic spiritual fornication, and spiritual adultery, that Jesus was confronting in his flock. They represented the worship of moral life instead of the giver of moral life.

How do you worship moral life?

Revelation 2:14 But I have a few things against thee, because thou hast there some that hold the teaching of Balaam, who taught Balak to cast a stumbling block before the children of Israel, to eat things sacrificed to idols, and to commit fornication.

But there are a couple of things you do that I don't like. You enlist the services of those who ostensibly are My servants but in truth are in religious community service for their financial prosperity (Balaam). Because of their greed, they serve the interests of your enemy, who will induce you to make a god out of purity, or wholeness, or morality, rather than Me (that is, to follow the Canaanite fertility cults). These leaders support the teachers of legalism knowing it will lead to your downfall and do so to curry favor with their flock.

That the fertility cults of the world are a symbolic representation of self-righteous legalism is a major concept in the bible. Worshipping fertility was worshipping life instead of the maker of life. When we are legalistic, we are because we have made a god out of the spiritual life we want, rather than the God who can give it to us. That makes God very angry because God loves us and wants us to know it. As long as we think we have to pay for God's provision of life with our deeds, we will never know He loves us. We will always believe God is mercenary, that He is like the john in the practice of ritual intercourse with the temple whore/priestess. Anyone who loves would feel the same revulsion God does in response to such a mindset in those they love and wish to pour their love out on.

Balaam is a symbol of those people who just want financial security. They aren't egotistical. They don't serve people out of a need to be worshipped by others like the Nicolaitans. They are just selfish in pursuing their material prosperity and safety. The Balaam in our Churches is leaders in a local community, who do not believe in legalism themselves, but who render their fellow believers vulnerable to teachers of legalism to ensure that they are financially secure. They know that they will be more socially popular, which translates into monetary (or social status) prosperity, if they preach or allow others to preach the legalism that is so deeply ingrained in the human soul.

Look at your churches to see who is teaching you to fixate on your lamentable moral condition. These are idolaters in Jesus' view. Now look to see if your leaders are supporting those false teachers. If so, they are probably, like Balaam, working out this betrayal of God's people for personal gain.

They sell out a pure trust in Jesus for legalism, for the money. Balaam was a prophet of the Lord, in ancient Canaan, who sold out his fellow worshippers of YHWH for money. His treason took the form of opening his fellow worshippers up to Baal worship, which would lead to their downfall because their enemy (their enemy and our enemy is ultimately Satan/pride) wanted their destruction and was willing to pay handsomely for it.

All three of these evil characters, Jezebel, Balaam, and the Nicolaitans, are primarily self-serving and spread disbelief in God's ability to govern man by the power of His spirit. And God gets mad when we even tolerate any of these three kinds of influences in our assemblies. He demands that we take a stand against them, that we oppose them decisively. When we fail to decisively stand against these three, it is because we have likewise failed to stand against self-righteousness within our hearts. We are what Jesus called double-minded.

God gave everything and withheld nothing of Himself in order to give us harmony (righteousness) with Him. He will not accept less than a total commitment from us in response. Such a total commitment takes the form of a decisive dependence upon the righteousness, the acceptable status, we have with God in Jesus, repudiating all legalism and trusting only in Jesus' sacrifice to make us one with God. As the hymn beautifully puts it, "*On Christ the solid rock I stand. All other ground is sinking sand.*"

The good news in all of this is that Jesus is being presented as He who will deal with these evil tendencies in us. We *do* have a Balaam within us, and only Jesus can effectively root him out.

Revelation 2:15 So hast thou also some that hold the teaching of the Nicolaitans in like manner.

This Balaam kind of self-righteousness is the same thing that's wrong with those personality-cult folks (the Nicolaitans), who get control over you by making you feel so guilty that you will, out of cowering shame, do anything they tell you to (which is basically to worship them to get relief).

You end up being seduced to want moral wholeness more than the God who can give you moral integrity by His spiritual power. Both Balaam and the Nicolaitans are sneaky in the way that they undermine your trust in God's ability to govern your dysfunctional soul by His spirit.

Both of these characters may be summed up as exploiting others' spiritual needs for selfish gain. Nicolaitans are, in contrast to Balaam, consumed by a desire for men's worship. This makes them become personality cult leaders, whose means of getting men's worship is to set themselves up as the sole distributor of the spiritual goods (the mediators between God and man, or between some ideal kind of life and us). They pose as experts, inherently superior to us and full of insight that we could never get directly from God ourselves. These emotionally damaged souls have always proliferated within human society.

Again. the core problem with these Nicolaitans is that they pose as mediators when only Jesus is given to us as a mediator between God and us. Only divine forgiveness can mediate between God and us. Anything else reinforces our species' delusional mindset of performance-based acceptance.

Revelation 2:16 Repent therefore; or else I come to thee quickly, and I will make war against them with the sword of my mouth.

Change your ways of accommodating them, of permitting them to teach in your community. Judge them, or I will come there and judge them directly. And you won't like the scene this causes because the reason you are too timid to conflict with them in the first place is that you care too much about your image (how others see you). And your image is too important to you because you don't really know who you are. Neither do the Nicolaitans. If you truly know who you are, you cannot be induced to sell out who you are, or need, like the Nicolaitans, to have others tell you who you are in expressions of worship of you.

Revelation 2:17 He that hath an ear, let him hear what the Spirit saith to the churches. To him that overcometh, to him will I give of the hidden manna, and I will give him a white stone, and upon the stone a new name written, which no one knoweth but he that receiveth it.

If you want to hear what God has to say to you, then listen to what His Spirit is saying to this ecclesia. If you listen to Me about this and conquer this tendency for selfishly committing spiritual treachery, I will feed you My proceeding word (manna), which is real spiritual life, and I will give you a new, divine sense of who you are (that is, a new name). You will become so secure in this identity you will no longer need anyone else to know who you are to feel completely worthy of existence. You will have *a name that no man knows* but you and me.

In being given a name written on a white stone, we are given an identity that is founded in a righteous/a *white* truth/*stone*. Can you guess what that righteous truth is? Yes, it is Jesus. Our name, our identity will be the bride, the embodiment of Jesus in this world. We will become sons and daughters of God in Jesus.

Thyatira Rev. 2:18-29

Revelation 2:18 And to the angel of the church in Thyatira write: These things saith the Son of God, who hath his eyes

like a flame of fire, and his feet are like unto burnished brass:

I, Jesus, am the Son of God, which means I am completely submitted to and in harmony with God. Therefore I have a perfectly pure perception of reality (eyes like fire) and a highly disciplined walk (feet like burnished bronze). Each church is given a key at the front door of Jesus' address to them. Thyatira is about to have their perceptions and walk judged/disciplined because Jesus means to shepherd us into full sonship with God.

Revelation 2:19 I know thy works, and thy love and faith and ministry and patience, and that thy last works are more than the first.

I can see that you have been serving others, and have loved others, and have trusted Me, and have been patient. I see also that you do more good now than you first did.

Sounds like a wonderful church to me. What could Jesus possibly find fault within these people?

Revelation 2:20 But I have this against thee, that thou sufferest the woman*(more accurately translated, your wife)*Jezebel, who calleth herself a prophetess; and she teacheth and seduceth my servants

to commit fornication, and to eat things sacrificed to idols.

To translate *sufferest that woman Jezebel* as **sufferest your wife Jezebel** is to characterize the leaders of the Church of Thyatira as King Ahab. King Ahab married this militant idolater, this missionary of self-righteous legalism to build alliances that might give him and his kingdom extra security. The evil in this behavior is twofold. First, we are to trust God to keep us safe. And second, we are not supposed to sell out the essential goodness of our trusting relationship with God by embracing a more popular self-righteous, self-trusting religion. This behavior is made to make us more acceptable to those whose human resources we faithlessly depend on instead of God. Do we Christian leaders today do this same kind of spiritual prostitution? Yes, we do. And Jesus will resolve this issue in us.

Jesus tells us, but the thing you do that I *truly* don't like is that you tolerate self-righteous teachers who teach you that one should embrace a self-righteous lust for wholeness (commit fornication with the gods and goddesses). This is *spiritual* fornication. In following legalism, you are being unfaithful to God and worshiping moral life instead of worshiping God. Remember, it is your view of things, your double-minded tolerance of legalism, that I am judging with My perfect view of things (with My eyes of fire), and your direction/your walk that I am judging with My righteous walk (with My feet of burnished bronze). You are going in the wrong direction; you have a faulty perception of what life in Jesus is all about. You are undecided about legalism, about walking in faith in Me, and about My power to effectively rule and transform your life.

Jezebel served another lord (Baal) and was militant in fighting for control of God's society. She was brutally coercive in making sure everyone else followed her Baal/her Lord. This is typical of teachers of self-righteousness. Jezebel craves control and cannot relax until she has it.

The first Jezebel was Eve after she was deceived. She was not content to have made her own self-destructive choice. She needed Adam to make the same choice. Eve's choice, like Jezebel's, was to feed on the knowledge of right and wrong, good and evil, to make this knowledge of right and wrong the basis of all her choices. The alternative to making choices based on a knowledge of right and wrong is to simply do what God tells us to do, without regard for whether it is right or wrong.

One must trust completely in God to have the degree of harmony with God necessary to be able to always do what He wants us to do. One cannot obey God's will, perfectly, completely, or perpetually, if one is attempting to do so out of fear of judgment from God. One must trust God's love to be their source of all they could ever need. Jesus did trust God completely, and thus Jesus is the Son of God.

Those of us who live by submission to the will of God, in the context of our trust in Jesus, are a dire threat to the Jezebel-like people in our churches because we do not make our choices based on a set of concepts about right and wrong as they do. And they viscerally hate us for that.

The Jezebel-like people garner control precisely by posing as the fount of wisdom concerning what is right and wrong in every situation. Thus, we who follow Jesus, and do only that which is of our Father, threaten Jezebel's control and the very purpose for Jezebel's existence (as being the final arbiter of what constitutes right and wrong in every situation). Jezebel picks right up where fallen Eve left off.

People who always consider what the right thing to do in every situation are never in submission to the will of God. They are governing their own lives utilizing their subjective human knowledge of right and wrong. Jezebel is militant and controlling, and to God, fiercely, and violently rebellious against His will and authority. God hates this fear-driven compulsion of a damaged human heart.

Jezebel is also associated with violent opposition to the prophets of the Lord. This aspect of her story symbolizes her militant opposition to people hearing from God themselves. This is a crucial thing to know about Jezebel. Self-righteous, legalistic people typically fear their minions having actual contact with God because it threatens their control. You see, everyone who is in harmonious contact with God becomes empowered by God. Jezebel will always move to undermine everyone else's connection and communication with God. They will warn us that our ability to hear from God is dangerously flawed (which it is), and then advise us to trust their supposedly more perfect ability to hear from God (which it isn't).

Hearing from God is an empowering thing for the hearer, and Jezebel, who equates power with control, does not want anyone but her to have such power. People with a Jezebel control issue typically vie for the role of being the last word in how the Bible (or God's will, or moral issues) should be understood. God wants us to trust His ability to communicate with us, regardless of our problems in hearing accurately.

People who have Jezebel's heart are people who have been sexually abused in childhood. Experiencing sexual abuse is a terrifying experience just because we can suddenly find ourselves terrifyingly out of control of a situation that ends in terrible wounding. We originally did not need to have this much control (before that horrible event happened to us), because up until that trauma we could trust people to behave like adults are supposed to behave around children; they are supposed to sacrifice the fulfillment of their own needs and desires to see to the fulfillment of a child's.

The enemy of our soul has taught us a lie about life through this kind of wounding experience, that we must control everyone else's desires. This kind of thinking is what is known today as a coping mechanism, and coping mechanisms *are always destructive* because they are based upon a faulty idea about life. It is this need to control everyone else's desires that induces Jezebel to make use of the tyranny of the guilty conscience in others.

Revelation 2:21 And I gave her time that she should repent; and she willeth not to repent of her fornication.

I, Jesus, have been telling those in your church who teach self-righteousness to stop for some time now. They won't.

Revelation 2:22 Behold, I cast her into a bed, and them that commit adultery with her into great tribulation, except they repent of her works.

God does not hate people who have Jezebel's heart. He understands that he/that she is simply trying to avoid the suppressed and unresolved terror of their childhood, and is doing so counterproductively and destructively by grasping for control. In Rev. 2:21-23 Jesus says that He has given Jezebel time to repent. This means that He has confronted her (probably through more than one person) and has given her time to repent, and if she does not repent, He still does not give up on her, He judges her.

His judgment on her is that He will cast her into a bed of tribulation, along with those who follow her. The bed of trouble/of tribulation that God casts Jezebel and her people into is to suddenly have all of her/their endeavors/which is *metaphorically speaking, her children* stop working for her. She clings to her projects because she puts her trust only in herself and so she wants the validation that her self-generated projects seem to give her.

Suffering great problems is God's merciful attempt at bringing healing to these people that have suffered great wounding in childhood, and as a result, crave control. In our great suffering, we inevitably experience ourselves having *no control* over our experience of pain. And in this experience of pain, over which we have no control, we can learn that we can let go of our need to control everything and everyone and trust God. And yes, all of us have a Jezebel in us. She's just more developed in some people.

Revelation 2:23 And I will kill her children with death; and all the churches shall know that I am he that searcheth the reins and hearts: and I will give unto each one of you according to your works.

And I will destroy all of the projects and ministries born out of this self-righteousness. I am the one to whom you must account for your choices (reins-kidneys) and your intentions (heart). I will know where you are truly coming from and will judge you; I promise you.

Revelation 2:24 But to you I say, to the rest that are in Thyatira, as many as have not this teaching, who know not the deep things of Satan, as they are wont to say; I cast upon you none other burden.

But to you who aren't buying their self-righteous teachings (who aren't as deeply initiated into their Fertility rites/their legalism and their attendant "*mysteries*", their esoteric religious concepts), putting up with their abuse is the only burden I will make you carry.

One of the ways Jezebel controls is to create an in-group, over which they rule. If you do not let her control you with her legalistic ways, she will kick you, unceremoniously, out of her in-group. These are the folks Jesus is addressing in this verse. We who follow Jesus are dramatically disinvited from those in-groups. We are not among their socially celebrated and empowered initiates. Having secret knowledge (Given by the leader and known only by members of the group) is also a control device typically used by Jezebels.

Revelation 2:25 Nevertheless that which ye have, hold fast till I come.

And whatever you do, hold fast to your trust in Me, and in My ability to rule your dysfunctional soul till I come. It will be tempting to leave your trust in Jesus to rule your life, so that you can join Jezebel's in-group, and end her scalding hatred of you, but do not do it.

Revelation 2:26 And he that overcometh, and he that keepeth my works unto the end, to him will I give authority over the nations:

If you conquer your tolerance of those self-righteous teachers and hold on to the gospel I give you, until the end (when I resolve your problems with the Jezebel within you, and externally in your church), I will appoint you to govern nations.

And you will rule them with power and effectiveness, just like a son and daughter of God is meant to do.

Revelation 2:28 and I will give him the morning star.

And I will see to it that you are given a divine sense of the timing of things (the Morning star by which people timed out the seasons) *[which is essentially another way of saying I will give you objectivity, insight]* so that you can rule well with wisdom. Wisdom/insight always displays a great sense of timing. Insight always knows what time it is. Wisdom is insight and is the morning star in our life. Insight is generated by an awareness of the context of that thing we need insight about. And God ultimately is the context of things. So, having harmonious trust restored to ur relationship with God naturally opens us up to much insight.

{Those who knew the stars were considered wise men. The morning star was a kind of calendar in the heavens, which told men when to plant their crops (by noting when it first appeared above the horizon in spring). The stars, the sun, and the moon were a symbol of enlightenment. Stars once enlightened us to what season in our life it currently was. This enlightenment is a metaphor for the insight we need to live out our lives productively.}

Revelation 2:29 He that hath an ear, let him hear what the Spirit saith to the churches.

If you, my followers, want to hear what God has to say to you, then listen to what His Spirit is saying to the ecclesia.

Thyatira trusted God to make them acceptable, in a general sort of way. But, they were conflicted about the extent of this acceptance so they entertained notions of self-righteousness too, which manifested as them tolerating the controlling Jezebel teachers. Thus, God was not the only one governing their actions. Fear of man was generally a problem for them. God is jealous of our total devotion to Him and won't tolerate anything less.

To encourage them to overcome their double-mindedness about whether God or they should govern their damaged souls, He told them that a full commitment to Jesus would result in God giving them His power to rule their souls, and not only their souls, but those of the nations as well. Talk about empowerment! And in the meantime, he was going to resolve their Jezebel heart issues.

What idolatry was in Old Covenant times, self-righteous legalism is in ours

Unless, and until, we get this concept, we will not become purified; we will not make ourselves ready for the Groom.

The scriptures very carefully define the development of self-righteousness, which has infected the human race since the fall. It is absolutely, and consistently, portrayed as the great evil, the ultimate threat to our species.

We have been given prime concepts such as rest (trust), and the sacrifice of a God-provided Lamb, from the outset to build a foundation for a new way of thinking. We have been warned that this new way of thinking is in opposition to the prevailing thinking of our species. We are shown, all the way through the entire scriptures, that there is a conflict between the older and younger brother. The older brother is a metaphor for a mentality of self-righteousness (because he was generally the one that was celebrated most in human society), and the younger brother is a metaphor for the mentality of righteousness, of trust (faith/belief) in the Lamb.

We are shown a nation (Israel) setting out in married life with God (in the Exodus from Egypt) with the prerequisite being an absolute trust in the blood of the Lamb, spread on the doorpost/covering the choices of their life. We see the death and rebirth of this nation in the wilderness as a result of their trust in this Lamb's blood.

We are given to believe that this young nation was not allowed to receive the land God promised to them and their forefathers until they died (via a 40-year tour of the desert) to the *distrusting* mindset that had developed in them over many generations of slavery. The land they were promised, we are informed, was known as the land of rest (and rest is a metaphor for *trust*). The Children of Israel had to undergo a spiritual rebirth to walk in this rest/trust in God. Slaves have a difficult time trusting anyone to love and care for them because few people ever do care for slaves. Yes, we are like those distrustful Israelite slaves in Egypt.

God, by His strength, sees to it that they begin to inherit this land of rest (trust). We are shown the back and forth war between this nation's trust in God and their blind trust in themselves, and that trust in God was the means God ordained for maintaining their presence in the land of plenty. This inner conflict is played out in their addiction to idols (icons of self-trust). It is a war depicted in terms of an ongoing bloody, messy, fight to the death. Deliverance from our inability to trust God does not happen all at once but must unfold via all of the drama God takes us through over the entire course of our existence.

Next, we are shown that this nation was overrun, overwhelmed, by the self-righteous (idolatrous) beliefs of the other nations and was consequently enslaved again. This state of being overrun by peer group pressure to embrace self-righteous legalism/idol worship is very familiar to us Christians, is it not? The difference between their enslavement at this time and their enslavement to Egypt is that they are now God's people, even though they have forgotten it. Does this remind you of anyone you know? I know I have often forgotten who I am in Jesus.

In all of this, we are shown the most amazing thing. The God who provided an ongoing working relationship between Himself and the nation of Israel has taken the responsibility to perfect His relationship with this people. Perfecting this relationship, we are told, involves teaching them who is boss (Lord), who they must account to, who they must fear, and who they must depend on. Jesus/Yashua means to lead us (Like Joshua led the children of Israel) into the land of rest.

We are informed that to achieve this perfecting of their trust in God, God will have to first destroy their trust in their own strength. By way of accomplishing this, Israel will come to see that even their moral and spiritual strength is inadequate. Toward this end, they will eventually come to experience themselves being so spiritually inadequate that they have even rejected the personification of God's governance (the Messiah), the Lamb of God.

This divine work to divest them of their trust in their own spiritual strength/integrity was ultimately manifested in their rejection of the Messiah. Daniel's prophesied event of God destroying the power of the holy people (via the destruction of the temple in Jerusalem), and the resulting dispersion of the Jewish population throughout the world resulted from this rejection. When we reject God, He leaves. God is love. Love will never force itself on another.

In the interest of driving the point home to them, God then picks another completely immoral and un-spiritual people to be His wife, to make Israel jealous and thus to return to Him. He does this on purpose, to show that He does not want man's self-generated integrity or morality. He wants our trust in Him. The only thing He will require of these people is that they depend on the Lamb's blood to make them acceptable to God. Jesus will similarly judge His church for their worship of moral wholeness.

Finally, to complete this work, God will have The Lamb, His Son, perfect the trust of these strange people in this kind of God-based relationship. The perfection of their trust in God will manifest in these people "loving not their soul unto death." In these strange people (which in time will include both Christians and Jews) is the proof, which completely convicts the world of her self-righteous distrust in God. The establishment of this evidence is the prerequisite to Jesus' judgment of the other nation's lack of trust. This is the whole enchilada.

After all of this is accomplished, God rules over a supremely harmonious universe.

THE ETERNAL END

Unless we get that the conflict is not between those who are moral and those who are immoral, is not between those who seek after pleasure and those who seek after purity, but is between those who are righteous/are in harmony with God, based on a gift of forgiveness from God, and those who think they are righteous, based on their works. Unless we get this point we will never begin to understand the Book of Revelation. More importantly, we will not have what it takes to get ready for our calling, which is to die like Jesus. We will be caught up in the storm at the end of this era and find ourselves persecuting those we wanted to be (the bride of Christ). And it won't matter how spiritual, how scripturally sound, or how committed to serving others you think you are. You WILL kill the trusters in God.

To avoid that fate, and to receive the fate of the believer, receive what Jesus says to all seven churches as being relevant to you. Ask Jesus to show you the Ephesus, Smyrna, Pergamum, Thyatira, Sardis, Philadelphia, and the Laodicea within you, and be filled with the repentance only God can generate in us.

Outcome -Sardis, Laodicea, Philadelphia

Therefore, I Will Sift The Chaff Of Hypocrisy, And Spiritual Pride, From You, Leaving Only A Mustard Seed Of Faithfulness To Remain

Sardis Rev. 3:1-6

Revelation 3:1 And to the angel of the church in Sardis write: These things saith he that hath the seven Spirits of God, and the seven stars:

Jesus is saying; I have control of (I hold) the leaders of My Churches. In case you don't realize it yet, you leaders report to Me. I'm your boss, not the people who pay your salary. He is saying this because they were so concerned about what people thought of them that they had lost sight of the fact that it was Jesus who employed them. These leaders (stars), and those they served, self-righteously, legalistically believed they had control of their life and, accordingly, their soul's restoration, but in truth, their life belonged to Jesus Who, accordingly, has the right and power to restore/to judge them.

I know thy works, that thou hast a name that thou livest, and thou art dead.

Revelation 3:2 Be thou watchful, and establish the things that remain, which were ready to die: for I have found no works of thine perfected before my God.

Do you smell something rotten? Cuz I sure do! I realize that people have come to believe your slick image, but it's putrid death to Me. You'd better get back to following Me (Jesus) and strengthen the things that remain un-strengthened because those dying parts of you will soon die completely. I say this to you because I have found no works in you that are a product of our relationship, no works that are a product of your trust in Jesus to lead you into wholeness and restoration. You are almost a completely nominal (in name only) Christian. You have the form of Christianity, but deny the divine power required to generate a Christian life. You are rank religious hypocrites!

It is almost universal among Christians to only see this Sardis Church in other Christian communities, and not in our own. I am chagrinned as I recall my own spiritually blind self-righteous judging of other Christians in this way. Yet there is a very Sardis-like Church in each one of us Christians, and it is important to become aware of it. The human species has what psychologists refer to as a public persona, a social mask that we wear when in public. We are not comfortable with other people knowing exactly who we are, and so we put on a mask when we are with them. Jesus did not have a public persona that was different from his private persona, and he didn't because He knew He was absolutely loved by God and so could trust God with his connection with his social herd. If some people, even those in positions of power, hated him, he felt no need to protect himself from their anger and contempt. His father in heaven was all the protection He needed. So, what you saw in Jesus was exactly who He was.

The rest of us humans, however, are amazingly developed, hypocrites. I am. You are. We all are wonderful mask-wearers. And the amount of mask-wearing we engage in is commensurate with how loved we feel we are by God. To the extent, we feel loved, with all of our dysfunction, by God, to that extent we are free to be the real us with other people.

And this is why this Sardis Church is being addressed by Jesus. They are not just hypocrites. They are fully committed to being hypocrites. In fact, they believe it is their Christian duty to be hypocrites. They would doubtless refer to this hypocrisy as them having a good Christian witness. The Sardis, mask-wearing person in you and I are equally committed to being a hypocrite, and we need to humbly face this miserable fact of our existence. Who can change this equation in our human condition? Jesus can. Only Jesus can. Only knowing that we are forgiven, and thus completely loved by God, can save us from this inner hypocrite impulse.

It is important to state that Jesus is not only what He represents to our species, in terms of divine forgiveness, but is also actually a divinely generated person who is authorized by God to restore God's creation to harmony with God. Jesus will, if you have given your life to Him, take your miserably, hypocrisy-burdened life through some very unpleasant healing. He will effectively rid you of your masks if you follow Him. And getting healed of our need for masks is to be a content, fully empowered, loving human. This kind of human existence is worth every bit of the suffering God deploys to give it to us.

One of the chief ways we followers of Jesus come to recognize one another in this world of hypocrites is that we are more capable of being real humans than most people are. As God makes us more real people, we come to spot others He has made real amongst the masses of dedicated mask-wearers. This is one of life's great pleasures.

Making our connection with our social herd more important than our connection with God is to engage in the idolatry of worship of our herd instinct. Idolatry was only ever us humans valuing something God made in us more than God. And we do this idolatry because we can no longer believe God loves us and would take care of our natural needs, like our need to fit within our social surroundings. Jesus fixes this little addiction to manically feeding our herd instinct by leading us into circumstances in which we have to do without those venerated social-herd connections. And if Jesus is more important to us than that very natural need to fit into a herd (now rendered unnatural by fear), then we will have to endure dying to this addiction until it is killed in us by Jesus. Enduring this kind of suffering with Jesus is how we come to *strengthen that which remains.*

Revelation 3:3 Remember therefore how thou hast received and didst hear; and keep it, and repent. If therefore thou shalt not watch, I will come as a thief, and thou shalt not know what hour I will come upon thee.

So turn completely around and go in the opposite direction you have been going in. Go in the direction of trusting Me, instead of trusting **you**, to restore your sick, dysfunctional soul to spiritual life. Trusting Me, Jesus, to have paid for your sins and to shepherd your weak, broken, dysfunctional soul into spiritual life is essentially the Gospel you first received from Me. Keep this message. If you don't, I will sneak into your life and silently steal what relationship you do have with Me away from you. And you won't even see Me coming, I promise you.

The thief imagery here is a good way to let us know that when we have thought to be our source of safety, by making a god out of our herd instinct, out of our connection to a social group, God will find a way to let us know that we are very unsafe. Being robbed by a thief is a very shocking way of letting us know we are not safe. The thief in this case is some event that happens to us that suddenly makes us aware that we no longer have a connection with God.

We thought we could have both gods. Now we are abruptly, shockingly made aware of the fact that we can't. We appeared to everyone as a person/as a church that was very religiously upright. And now we are suddenly exposed as the Godless hypocrites we are. Now everyone knows we never were actually who we pretended to be. This kind of divine theft is more common than you think. I can tell you I have experienced it. You probably have too.

So, this means, we will either let God take us through the suffering of losing our addictive connection with our social group (thus liberating us to be genuine people) up front, or we will later on experience Jesus destroying those very social connections we worshiped, and our connection with God too.

Revelation 3:4 But thou hast a few names in Sardis that did not defile their garments: and they shall walk with me in white; for they are worthy.

But a few of you there are living by genuine trust in Me. I will clean up your life (I will restore your trust in God so that He shines through you in love and genuineness) because you deserve it for trusting Me.

Revelation 3:5 He that overcometh shall thus be arrayed in white garments; and I will in no wise blot his name out of the book of life, and I will confess his name before my Father, and before his angels.

To those of you who overcome your hypocrisy (the worship of your public image, and by extension your social connections), I will clean up your life, and I will fully accept you (enter your name in the book of life). Entering our name in the book of life is to give us a whole new identity. This identity Jesus will give us is the same one He had. We become God's beloved sons and daughters that He is very pleased with. And this identity of God's beloved children renders us, like Jesus, very genuine people.

And I will bring you home to meet Dad and the family (confess his name before My Father and His angels). This is a wonderful way of saying that Jesus will bring you into complete intimate harmony with God. In case you can't tell, conquering the impulse to be a hypocrite really turns Jesus on.

Revelation 3:6 He that hath an ear, let him hear what the Spirit saith to the churches.

If you want to hear what God has to say to you, then listen to what His Spirit is saying to the ecclesia.

Philadelphia Rev. 3:7-13

When you get to the ecclesia of Philadelphia, you get the feeling that Jesus is so joyful and excited about this group that He is hitting the ground running as He begins to speak.

Revelation 3:7 And to the angel of the church in Philadelphia write: These things saith he that is holy, he that is true, he that hath the key of David, he that openeth and none shall shut, and that shutteth and none openeth:

To-tal-ly de-vo-ted to you.

I, Jesus, am a humble, trustworthy, authority. You know, the kind of thing God is determined to empower no matter what, like God empowered humble King David (I have the key of David). Jesus is saying this to His people in Philadelphia because they have also humbly trusted God with their soul's restoration, like David, in the gaudy shadow of those King Saul-like prideful Christians who are arrogantly self-righteous.

Revelation 3:8 I know thy works (behold, I have set before thee a door opened, which none can shut), that thou hast a little power, and didst keep my word, and didst not deny my name.

Yes, I know all about the work you do. I have given you God's anointing/ His authority and empowering (an open door is an expression of this empowerment), which no one, and nothing, can oppose because you keep My word and don't deny My name.

This group of followers of Jesus had but a little power. They had little social influence (which is a kind of power) and little material power to change the things that were wrong with their life. The legalistic people who claimed to be believers in God, but were actually in rebellion with God (were a synagogue/church of Satan), who looked for all the world to have conquered all of their social and material problems. These rebels were the ones who everybody admired and respected as being spiritually mature, who everybody gave a high social position to, and who everybody supported and encouraged and catered to throughout their life. And they decisively marginalized those that followed Jesus humbly into suffering's transformation.

People often mistake material blessing or social celebrity for being God's blessing. It happened then, and it happens a lot now, too. In the apostle

John's time, these people were their Jewish Christian brothers who were self-righteous and were prospering financially and socially. In our time it is those Christian brothers and sisters who will not receive Jesus as their righteousness with God. They militantly cling to their legalism instead, and the rebellious self-governance this is an expression of. And the financial and social wealth that camouflages their rebellion is not only material and social prosperity but is also the seeming psychological/emotional health that they publicly display, while those that follow Jesus display all of the hideous issues Jesus is bringing to the surface in them to heal and liberate them from those issues.

Yet you, beloved of the Lord (like David), have little power, and you suffer like David did when under the haughty, persecuting, rebellious hand of King Saul (like the religious establishment of Philadelphia). And like David, you did not take matters into your hand and attempt to gain power for yourself. You humbled yourself under the mighty hand of God, and now God is going to exalt you and humble those who oppressed you.

This *Philadelphian* lack of power is the powerlessness to fix our publicly visible problems in the presence of those haughty hypocrites, who judge us and persecute us for our lack of power, wrongly suggesting that our lack of power is God's punishment upon us. **It is a kind of suffering that all who follow Jesus are called to.** It is not pleasant, but it yields the enormous empowerment that God gives those who humble themselves under His hand. We are all asked to suffer this David-like painful indignity because there is a part of every one of us that is in agreement with those pride-filled ones. And only by suffering their abuse can we die to that pride in us.

Know this, it Is Only Ever Our Pride That Limits God's Empowering Of Us. No person or persons ever will be able to hinder or stop God's will to empower us.

Revelation 3:9 Behold, I give of the synagogue of Satan, of them that say they

are Jews, and they are not, but do lie; behold, I will make them to come and worship before thy feet, and to know that I have loved thee.

Look! I'm going to make those churches full of spiritually rebellious people, who say they are Jews/Christians but aren't, the liars; I will make them worshipfully submit to your way of walking life out *(worship before your feet)*. They will come around to believing in the integrity of your way of living in dependence upon Me. And I will make them know you are loved by Me.

Wow! That's pretty intense, isn't it? Jesus is filled with a passionate love for these trusters.

Revelation 3:10 Because thou didst keep the word of my patience, I also will keep thee from the hour of trial, that hour which is to come upon the whole world, to try them that dwell upon the earth.

Because you accepted what I modeled for you, that real trust requires patient endurance of suffering in the face of persecution, I will keep you from the judgment, which everyone else on earth will have to go through. You will be killed and resurrected (or raptured) before the time of worst trouble comes, and won't have to live through all that terror and pain.

Revelation 3:11 I come quickly: hold fast that which thou hast, that no one take thy crown.

Hang on to Me, beloved. I won't be long now. Just continue trusting Me. And don't let anyone tell you you're crazy for trusting. In this way, you will receive the tremendous anointing/crown/empowerment I have prepared for you.

Revelation 3:12 He that overcometh, I will make him a pillar in the temple of my God, and he shall go out thence no more: and I will write upon him the name of my God, and the name of the city of my God, the new Jerusalem, which cometh down out of heaven from my God, and mine own new name.

If you conquer, by holding onto Me in the face of your suffering powerlessness, I will make you into an arch-example (pillar) for all people in the world. They will learn, from looking at your life, how to respond to God. You will have your place established eternally within God's ruling administration (you will never go out). And you will be strongly identified with God, with His spiritual culture (the new Jerusalem), and with Me (You will have His name). You will no longer be associated in people's minds with being a social-economic loser. When people think of you, they will automatically associate you with what God and what I, Jesus, achieve.

Notice the people God has already given us as our examples. He has taken these very ordinary humans and made their lives eternally celebrated. Whatever they had to give up in trusting in God, God has more than made up for in His rewarding of them. Jesus is telling us God will do this for us as well if we too endure the suffering Jesus takes us through (at the hands of the socially celebrated self-righteous).

Revelation 3:13 He that hath an ear, let him hear what the Spirit saith to the churches.

If you want to hear what God has to say to you, then listen to what His Spirit is saying to the ecclesia.

Allow me to sum up this word to the Church of Philadelphia. I think it bears repeating.

Those of us who have been appointed to sit next to the self-righteous, those who are given position and favor by men, and hear them judge us for not being as prosperous as them, and suffer financial and psychological and emotional, and social hardships while your counterparts thrive in luxury and ease, you are told to hold onto Jesus, because Jesus comes quickly, and He will right this situation when He comes.

And He also reminds us that even though we lack all manner of social and financial empowerment, we have already been anointed by God in ways that the self-righteous never dreamed of. We are told that God has opened doors for us in which to function in this anointing, even though we have been regularly oppressed, suppressed, and marginalized by those spiritually rebellious people who are currently thriving in positions of social and financial power.

Jesus tells us that He will vindicate us from these oppressors in the most wonderful way. He will make them acknowledge that the way we have been trusting in God is the true, the best way to live, and He will make them realize and confess publicly that God has loved us, who were so frequently and wrongfully judged as being out of God's favor because of the hardships we were enduring.

Finally, Jesus tells us that if we conquer by holding fast to Him till He comes, He will make an example of us, like He has the men and women of the bible. We will become an eternal pillar of God's community, a standard of trust, which God will use to encourage others to trust for all of the years to come.

Many of us who have put our trust in Jesus, instead of our human strength, have had many problems and dire needs (like emotional problems, psychological problems, social problems, and financial problems) while those around us seemingly thrived and looked down on us for these problems and needs. Jesus is telling us that it is we who He is passionately in love with because we have been suffering these things for Him, trusting Him to fix what needs fixing in us, instead of trusting in our human strength like most everyone else. The self-righteous have merely hidden their many problems from view.

Typically, those of us in this Philadelphian state of mind tend to partially agree with our accusers and think our suffering is due to our flawed humanity. Jesus is reminding us that our facing these weaknesses in us is due to our loving Jesus more than our comfort and ease, and to hold onto Jesus. He will swiftly and wonderfully overturn this situation when He comes. This divine vindication and annointing will be in this present age. And it will carry over into the next age.

Laodicea Rev. 3:14-22

Revelation 3:14 And to the angel of the church in Laodicea write: These things saith the Amen, the faithful and true witness, the beginning of the creation of God:

Jesus is saying to those of you in the Laodicean condition (that is, to all of us): You need to know, I don't lie, and I am the origin of all life. You need Me to say this to you, because you apparently don't know where your life comes from (God the creator), and that I don't lie when I promise you something (faithful and true), like the restoration of your soul. This has consequently rendered you false, and empty of life.

Revelation 3:15 I know thy works, that thou art neither cold nor hot: I would thou wert cold or hot.

I know your deeds. I know that you are hypocrites (lukewarm). I would rather you do what you want, whether it is good or evil than hypocritically act like you are doing what I want when your heart is not in it. That is being lukewarm in your commitment to Jesus' Lordship. As someone in my church community pointed out, one only wants to drink hot or cold things. No one wants to drink something lukewarm. Jesus is revolted by our hypocrisy.

Jesus is saying to us that He would rather we were walking openly and honestly before Him and were doing what we wanted while constantly trusting Him to change our hearts to want what He wants for us. How many of us do this? How many of us even believe Jesus wants us to trust Him to govern us by His spirit? How many of us truly believe God does not want us to trust in our flesh (our human strength) to govern our human issues? How many of us trust in *"Will Power"* instead of God's power to change our behavior and then sew God's label on our efforts after the fact?

To live any other way is to be a hypocrite who washes the outside of the cup, but leaves the inside full of corruption, a hypocrite who whitewashes (superficially heals our past emotional wounds (sepulcher) and the misbehavior this generates in us, while inside we are full of the rotting impulses engendered by our unresolved memories (*that is, we are tombs full of dead men's bones*). We pretty up our heart's motives, we rationalize and justify, and deny our heart's true condition.

You have become indifferent to My rule because you don't believe Me when I say I can restore you by the power of My spirit, and that I AM the source of your spiritual life. You have come to trust in your strength.

Oh, how full of this spiritual corruption we humans are!

Observe What Jesus Says To The Self-Righteous, Legalistic Hypocrites Of His Day.

Allow me to bring up Jesus' confronting of the religious leaders of His day in Matthew 23. By doing this I hope you can see how consistent what God revealed to the apostle John is with what Jesus preached. It is seamlessly joined to Jesus' gospel.

Matthew. 23:1 Then spake Jesus to the multitudes and to his disciples, 2 saying, The scribes and the Pharisees sit on Moses' seat: 3 all things therefore whatsoever they bid you, these do and observe: but do not ye after their works; for they say, and do not.

Do what they tell you to do, as far as moral behavior is concerned, because they are making use of divine principles given us through Moses, but don't do as they do, for they are hypocrites. Fulfill the laws that they teach, but don't follow their example.

4 Yea, they bind heavy burdens and grievous to be borne, and lay them on men's shoulders; but they themselves will not move them with their finger.

The law is a heavy burden that is grievous to be borne, and they love to bind you to this law, while they will not make the least effort to help you fulfill these same laws. The law is grievous to be carried out because there are so many aspects of our humanity that do not truly know God loves us. The self-righteous do not care that you don't know God loves you. They just want to tell you you are breaking God's law. Helping you know God loves you would be them lifting a finger to help you fulfill the law.

5 But all their works they do to be seen of men: for they make broad their phylacteries, and enlarge the borders *of their garments*, 6 and love the chief place at feasts, and the chief seats in the synagogues, 7 and the salutations in the marketplaces, and to be called of men, Rabbi.

The reason they won't lift a finger to help you fulfill God's law is that they are just hypocrites. All of their behavior and deeds are done only to make themselves look good to other people. They don't ever truly fulfill the law but only merely seem to. Because this is so, they make a great show of their religiousness (make broad their phylacteries) and love positions of honor at festivities and church meetings. They love salutations in the marketplaces, and to be called reverend/doctor/pastor/rabbi/father. They have chosen the acceptance of men over the unconditional love of God, their father.

8 But be not ye called Rabbi: for one is your teacher, and all ye are brethren. 9 And call no man your father on the earth: for one is your Father, *even* he who is in heaven. 10 Neither be ye called masters: for one is your master, *even* the Christ.

But you, My followers, don't have anyone call you professor/doctor/pastor/rabbi/father, etc. Your identity should exclusively be that of a fellow brother or sister. Take no social status above anyone else, whatsoever. As My followers you have all been granted the highest status possible for a human being, you are sons and daughters of God. Likewise, don't ever let anyone call you a mentor, because you are all being actively mentored by Me.

It is amazing just how much we humans fail to see what Jesus is saying in this verse. How rare it is that a servant of God comes to serve dressed only in the righteousness of Jesus, with no credentials or titles. I know of very few people who do this. And yet Jesus makes a big point of this issue. I should point out that I also fail to do this in ways I am unaware of. There are many covert ways we guild the Lilly so that people will receive what we offer, and do not know we are doing so.

11 But he that is greatest among you shall be your servant. 12 And whosoever shall exalt himself shall be humbled, and whosoever shall humble himself shall be exalted.

Instead of high social status, you who follow Me will prize serving others. And you will trust God to empower you; not men. You will come to know that whoever exalts himself will get humbled by God, and whoever humbles himself will get exalted by God. You will know this because God will have humbled the prideful you. If you truly follow Jesus, you leave behind all social status except that of a follower of Jesus and a son or daughter of God. You won't need or want or accept any other social status when you follow Jesus.

This should tell you how little we truly follow Jesus, and how much we have been following other men. And yet, Jesus is standing right there, waiting for you to follow Him. You can do so at any time, but doing so will cost you. It will cost you your man-generated social status for sure. If you have ever fallen in love with Jesus after feeling His love for you, this will be viewed as a great trade-off to you. If you haven't, or if you have left your first love of Christ's forgiveness, it will be unbearable.

Regardless of whether you see giving up your social status to follow Jesus as a great tradeoff, or an unbearable burden, for all of us, giving up our social status to follow Jesus, will feel like a social death, one that will be quite unpleasant.

The following passage in Matthew 19 defines Jesus' position on the relative difficulty the rich (prosperous in money and social status) have in following Jesus (entering the Kingdom of God). Note that although we humans can't overcome this difficulty, Jesus says God can overcome this difficulty that the rich must deal with. God simply renders the wealthy poor, by His grace, and then they too are able to follow Jesus. All who have come to follow Jesus have been rendered aware of their poverty by God. Only the sick need a doctor, Jesus said. It is God's grace that makes us able to see our real poverty and sickness, to understand how far we've fallen from sonship to God. If you find yourself bound by apathy toward God, know that this is a product of you not yet knowing your poverty. You are presently deluded into thinking your self-generated thriving is truly thriving. Ask God to show you it isn't. He will, and He will do this out of love for you.

It is our riches, our successes, and our moral achievements that impoverish our souls. It takes a great and merciful God to deliver us from them. ***"With men this is impossible, but with God all things are possible."***

Matt. 19:16 And behold, one came to him and said, Teacher, what good thing shall I do, that I may have eternal life? 17 And he said unto him, Why askest thou me concerning that which is good? One there is who is good: but if thou wouldest enter into life, keep the commandments. 18 He saith unto him, Which? And Jesus said, Thou shalt not kill, Thou shalt not commit adultery, Thou shalt not steal, Thou shalt not bear false witness, 19 Honor thy father and thy mother; and, Thou shalt love thy neighbor as thyself. 20 The young man saith unto him, All these things have I observed: what lack I yet? 21 Jesus said unto him, If thou wouldest be perfect, go, sell that which thou hast, and give to the poor, and thou shalt have treasure in heaven: and come, follow me. 22 But when the young man heard the saying, he went away sorrowful; for he was one that had great possessions.

Matt. 19:23 And Jesus said unto his disciples, Verily I say unto you, It is hard for a rich man to enter into the kingdom of heaven. 24 And again I say unto you, It is easier for a camel to go through a needle's eye, than for a rich man to enter into the kingdom of God. 25 And when the disciples heard it, they were astonished exceedingly, saying, Who then can be saved? 26 And Jesus looking upon them said to them, With men this is impossible; but with God all things are possible. 27 Then answered Peter and said unto him, Lo, we have left all, and followed thee; what then shall we have? 28 And Jesus said unto them, Verily I say unto you, that ye who have followed me, in the regeneration when the Son of man shall sit on the throne of his glory, ye also shall sit upon twelve thrones, judging the twelve tribes of Israel. 29 And every one that hath left houses, or brethren, or sisters, or father, or mother, or children, or lands, for my name's sake, shall receive a hundredfold, and shall inherit eternal life. 30 But many shall be last that are first; and first that are last.

No one should feel better than others because of their social status. God has a thing about picking the last to be first, not because they are somehow better than anyone else, but because in doing so He can correct our blindness concerning the part He intends to play in the restoration of our soul. By picking those that human society despises, or is embarrassed by, to restore first, He makes the statement that He does not need our human virtues or our integrity; He needs our trusting, yielded heart.}

Matt. 23:13 But woe unto you, scribes and Pharisees, hypocrites! because ye shut the kingdom of heaven against men: for ye enter not in yourselves, neither suffer ye them that are entering in to enter.

But as for you religious leaders who don't follow Me, you hypocrites; trouble be upon you! Trouble be upon you because you keep people from knowing that God can govern them by His spirit, and neither will you let God govern you by His spirit. In doing this you shut the kingdom (and kingship) of God against men. Jesus speaks trouble to our self-righteous, legalistic lives. And Jesus is the eternal word of God; the word that speaks everything into being, and which holds everything in existence together. If Jesus speaks trouble to us, we will have trouble. I can tell you that I have certainly had much trouble and that it was given me to counter the self-righteous man in me. Jesus is faithful and kind even to us self-righteous hypocrites.

Matt. 23:14 Woe to you, scribes and Pharisees, hypocrites! For you devour widows' houses, and for a pretense make long prayers. Therefore you will receive greater condemnation.

You religious leaders who don't follow Me; trouble be upon you, because you exploit the vulnerability of the poor and helpless, and do so in the name of service to God. Because you do this evil in the name of service to God, you will receive greater condemnation from God (God does not appreciate you associating His name with your evil deeds).

Matt. 23:15 Woe unto you, scribes and Pharisees, hypocrites! for ye compass sea and land to make one proselyte; and when he is become so, ye make him twofold more a son of hell than yourselves.

You religious leaders who don't follow Me, hypocrites; trouble be upon you because you search the world over to find one convert, and when you find him you turn him into twice the product of unresolved issues in the heart that you are (son of hell/Hades, the place of the dead, which symbolizes man's heart of unresolved past experiences with pain and wounding fear).

Matt. 23:16 Woe unto you, ye blind guides, that say, Whosoever shall swear by the temple, it is nothing; but whosoever shall swear by the gold of the temple, he is a debtor. 17 Ye fools and blind: for which is greater, the gold, or the temple that hath sanctified the gold? 18 And, Whosoever shall swear by the altar, it is nothing; but whosoever shall swear by the gift that is upon it, he is a debtor. 19 Ye blind: for which is greater, the gift, or the altar that sanctifieth the gift? 20 He therefore that sweareth by the altar, sweareth by it, and by all things thereon. 21 And he that sweareth by the temple, sweareth by it, and by him that dwelleth therein. 22 And he that sweareth by the heaven, sweareth by the throne of God, and by him that sitteth thereon.

You religious leaders who don't follow Me, you blind guides; trouble be upon you because you say that a person's testimony, when sworn to by the temple, is not binding, but if he swears to it by the gold in the temple, it is. You fixate upon what you must do to spiritually prosper and remain ignorant of what God must do for you. Which is greater, the gold or the temple that renders it sacred? What is more valuable, the stuff you bring to God, or the stuff God brings to you?

Likewise, you say that a person's testimony is not binding if he swears by the altar, but it is as if he swears by the gift upon the altar. You willfully ignorant and spiritually blind people, which is more important, the gift or the alter that renders it sacred? You confuse the part God plays in our connection with Him (His alter) with the part we play (our sacrifice/gift/ service).

Thus, whoever swears by the alter, automatically swears by the gift laid upon it, and he who swears by the temple automatically swears by it, and he who lives there, just as he who swears by heaven also swears by God who reigns there. If you confuse God's part with your part, you will not know that making God your focus is how you will be enabled to do your part.

Matt. 23:23 Woe unto you, scribes and Pharisees, hypocrites! for ye tithe mint and anise and cummin, and have left undone the weightier matters of the law, justice, and mercy, and faith: but these ye ought to have done, and not to have left the other undone. 24 Ye blind guides, that strain out the gnat, and swallow the camel!

You religious leaders who don't follow Me, hypocrites; trouble be upon you, because you tithe mint and anise and cumin, and leave undone the more important laws of human behavior. You are blind mentors that strain at a gnat and swallow a camel! You fixate on insignificant issues and altogether miss the important issues.

Again, if we focus on our part, and not on God's part, we will be blind to God and what is truly important. The self-righteous only care about their relationship with men (their social position).

In Jesus' address to the Churches, we can see exactly what kind of woe/ trouble Jesus will bring upon us to judge us. The trouble will come to us all because we are all those self-righteous Pharisees. Yet, if we embrace, if we receive this trouble as coming to us from Jesus (instead of believing it is coming from Satan or men, which we all tend to do) then we will be transformed and empowered by that trouble. If we don't accept it as being from God, that same trouble will destroy us.

Matt. 23:25 Woe unto you, scribes and Pharisees, hypocrites! for ye cleanse the outside of the cup and of the platter, but within they are full from extortion and excess. 26 Thou blind Pharisee, cleanse first the inside of the cup and of the platter, that the outside thereof may become clean also. 27 Woe unto you, scribes and Pharisees, hypocrites! for ye are like unto whited sepulchres, which outwardly appear beautiful, but inwardly are full of dead men's bones, and of all uncleanness. 28 Even so ye also outwardly appear righteous unto men, but inwardly ye are full of hypocrisy and iniquity.

You religious leaders who don't follow Me, hypocrites; trouble be upon you because you clean the surface of your life and leave the inside filthy and full of rotting moral corruption. Your morality is superficial because you won't deal with your real issues, your internal emotional issues. In using the cup/platter metaphor, Jesus is symbolically pointing to their superficial service to others. A cup is used for service. In bringing up the sepulcher, Jesus is symbolically pointing to the superficial handling of their problems in their wicked heart. A sepulcher is a place of past/of dead issues in our life. Their heart is full of unresolved emotional issues *(rotting flesh)*, and thus their posing as moral human beings is just that, posing.

Matt. 23:29 Woe unto you, scribes and Pharisees, hypocrites! for ye build the sepulchers of the prophets, and garnish the tombs of the righteous, 30 and say, If we had been in the days of our fathers, we should not have been partakers with them in the blood of the prophets. 31 Wherefore ye witness to yourselves, that ye are sons of them that slew the prophets. 32 Fill ye up then the measure of your fathers.

You religious leaders who don't follow Me, hypocrites; trouble be upon you because you preach lofty sermons about the servants of God who have come before you and suffered and died for their relationship with God (garnish the tombs of the righteous), saying; if we had lived back then, we would have not acted like those who came before us, who killed them. In saying this you thus testify that you are like them who killed the servants of God. So, do as much murdering of the prophets of God as those who came before you, then. When we cannot face our internal filth/our fears, unbelief, and pride we cannot benefit from the examples God places in the scriptures of God saving man from human dysfunction. We distance ourselves from those evil people in the bible, and then cannot come to see that God can resolve our evil issues.

How many of us have read about the wicked children of Israel, who would not enter into God's rest, would not trust God regardless of how many miracles God showed them, and thought, I would not have been like them? I would have trusted God. When we take this approach to those accounts in the bible, we are being hypocrites, and are blind to just how dysfunctional we are. We all have to deal with the same degree of unbelief that the collective children of Israel did. The ratio of belief to unbelief is not very high for any of us. We really do only begin with a mustard seed amount of trust in God, and it is God who builds our trust in Him by taking us through our own wilderness journey.

All of us need to read those biblical accounts of unbelief and humble ourselves before God, asking Him to show us where we are unbelieving just like them. But if you care more about your relationship with men than your relationship with God, you will never do this.

Matt. 23:33 Ye serpents, ye offspring of vipers, how shall ye escape the judgment of hell?

You people who are deceivers and deceived, who are wise in your own eyes, how will you escape the judgments coming to your heart's unresolved wounds (and the destructive behaviors this wounding generates, this judgment of succumbing to behavior from hell/Hades, from your un-faced corrupt heart)? Only by pursuing a harmonious connection with God can you (or any of us) hope to see that wounding in our heart be healed, and delivered from the compulsive drive to do those destructive things we humans do because of our wounded past. You humans cannot even begin to sort through and resolve the massive amount of emotional damage in your life.

Matt. 23:34 Therefore, behold, I send unto you prophets, and wise men, and scribes: some of them shall ye kill and crucify; and some of them shall ye scourge in your synagogues, and persecute from city to city: 35 that upon you may come all the righteous blood shed on the earth, from the blood of Abel the righteous unto the blood of Zachariah son of Barachiah, whom ye slew between the sanctuary and the altar. 36 Verily I say unto you, All these things shall come upon this generation.

Therefore, I will personally send to you your own set of prophets to kill, and wise men and teachers sent from Me. Some of them you will kill and have executed. Some of them you will berate and oppress in your religious institutions and religious communities and will persecute them wherever they go once they leave your communities.

Of course, we do not kill them in today's civilized world. We just marginalize them, or destroy their reputation, by slandering them. But the effect is the same. This will happen so that you will be found guilty of the blood of every righteous martyr from the blood of Abel the righteous to Zachariah, son of Barachiah, who you slew right in the face of God (between the sanctuary and the altar). Yep, this goes for us as much as it did the self-righteous people of Jesus' day. Truly, I say to you religious leaders who will not follow Me, I will see to it that these things will come to your lives.

I have slandered God's servants, too. In my pride and envy, I allowed myself the freedom to judge the intentions and achievements of others as not being from God, when it was. And, yes, I truly believed I was right in my judgments of them, at that time. Of course, that does not matter to God. He still does not like it when we do this. This prideful judgment came from my own self-righteous hypocrisy.

Ask God to show you where you have done this same thing. It will only bring your more humble security in His love and providence if you do.

Because we delusionally believe we are different from the evil people out there, and the evil people back then, God will send to us the same kind of circumstances that triggered those people out there to do evil, and that triggered those people back then to do evil. And you will be forced to face that you indeed are exactly like them. There are no good or evil kinds of people. There are only massively damaged humans in need of God to fix their damaged lives.

Jesus is saying this to the religious leaders of our day as much as He was saying it to the religious leaders of 2000 years ago. And He is saying it to the religious people of today as well.

Matt. 23:37 O Jerusalem, Jerusalem, that killeth the prophets, and stoneth them that are sent unto her! how often would I have gathered thy children together, even as a hen gathereth her chickens under her wings, and ye would not! 38 Behold, your house is left unto you desolate. 39 For I say unto you, Ye shall not see me henceforth, till ye shall say, Blessed is he that cometh in the name of the Lord.

Oh religious establishment, oh religious establishment, that kills those that serve and account to God (and not man), who publicly condemn those I have sent to warn you to repent, how often would I have brought your followers (and the immature parts of your religious person's soul) under My nurturing rule, like a hen, gathers her chicks, but you wouldn't let them come to Me!

Behold, your religious establishment is left to you desolate, lifeless, and spiritually dead. God will utterly destroy the established ways we self-righteously try to govern our human condition and our human communities with.

Because of what I am going to do to you, I now say to you that you will not see salvation (Me/Jesus) again until you value your relationship with God so highly that you will choose to say, Blessings upon anyone who comes to us sent from God.

Jesus wants us, who are in positions of responsibility, of oversight of the spiritual welfare of others, to be so hungry for God that we will humbly be open to anyone who comes to us from God. What most church leaders do today is only receive those that are from their church system or those they have personally sought out, or those men have credentialled and celebrated.

 Church leadership will seldom receive a servant of God, who God has sent to warn them of their need to repent. They will typically give all manner of justification for not receiving them. They will either give them the cold shoulder, and hope that they go away, or outright tell them that they won't receive them because they don't recognize their authority to come with a message of repentance. The religious leadership in churches today is very much like that of Jesus' day.

And the Church leadership is exactly like the self-righteous governing mindset in each of us individual Christians. It brutally suppresses God's wooing of us. Do not think this is not true of you. It is. It is true of every human. Yet, Jesus has the cure for us human Pharisees. This bold, harsh passage in Mathew 23 is meant to be good news for those of us that know we humans are highly developed hypocrites. Yet what we tend to think when we read this is; Yes, Jesus, get those Pharisees! We do not know that we *ARE* those Pharisees. All of us are. I am. You are, too.

Again, let me say that it is important for all who read this (whether we are leaders or not) to humble themselves before God, confessing, "I am these hypocrites"; God, show me where this applies to me. Believe me, God will show you, and when He does you will experience deep, rich, Godly sorrow, which can lead to life-changing repentance. If you won't humble yourself in this way, Jesus has already pronounced judgment on you in this address to the religious leaders in the religious establishment of His day.

Let me, John Brusseau, publicly confess that I am one of these spiritually blind religious leaders; I am a hypocritical Laodicean. For example, I have pridefully put myself in front of people in such a way that I have lifted myself up and consequently obscured, God.

God, continue to show me where I am self-righteous and legalistic, where I am a spiritually blind leader of men so that I can effectively repent, and become the son of God, and brother, in Christ, that you have called me to be.

Revelation 3:16 So because thou art lukewarm, and neither hot nor cold, I will spew thee out of my mouth.

Because you won't decide who you will trust to rule your troublesome humanity and are thus being a hypocrite, I will decide for you. I'm dramatically leaving you. I have experienced this drama in my own life, many times. It's not fun. Recall those times in your life in which you allowed yourself to react out of defensiveness to someone. You were adamant. Note how God let your *noble* efforts blow up in your face. What Jesus is saying He will do to the Laodicean Church leaders is just like that. It is truly very dramatic what Jesus does to kill off the lukewarm aspects of us.

Revelation 3:17 Because thou sayest, I am rich, and have gotten riches, and have need of nothing; and knowest not that thou art the wretched one and miserable and poor and blind and naked:

Here's what I'm talking about; you say you have lots of moral integrity, and that you have made yourselves right with God by the things you have done. You're not. You don't realize you're highly dysfunctional and unhappy, spiritually impoverished, without spiritual insight, and uncovered (un-provided for and unprotected) by Me. And this is because you are so full of your human providence.

Revelation 3:18 I counsel thee to buy of me gold refined by fire, that thou mayest become rich; and white garments, that thou mayest clothe thyself, and that the shame of thy nakedness be not made manifest; and eyesalve to anoint thine eyes, that thou mayest see.

I strongly advise you to look to Me for the trust/faith you need (Gold is a metaphor for faith/trust. It is the only thing we can truly spend to get what we need from God), so that you can see what I can accomplish in getting your act together. I long to give you a deep sense of how completely God accepts you and can restore you, so that your whole perception of life is renewed (eye salve), and you start seeing the real world, the world I designed you to live in and be a part of. I will make you able to see that you can trust God to be the source of everything you need to survive and thrive.

Revelation 3:19 As many as I love, I reprove and chasten: be zealous therefore, and repent.

EVERYONE whom I love, I speak harshly to and put through My hard training. *I underlined EVERYONE here because it cannot be overstated that this applies to us all.* So, passionately change your course. Jesus is saying to us; I would not say this to you unless I loved you, so listen to Me, and change your direction.

Revelation 3:20 Behold, I stand at the door and knock: if any man hear my voice and open the door, I will come in to him, and will sup with him, and he with me.

Look. I want to come into the house of your soul, into your life. I'm knocking, knocking. If you let Me (and My kind of harmonious trust in God) come into your soul house (your life), I will have intimate fellowship with you. We will feed on spiritual, life-giving, life-changing, truth together.

If you find that you do not feel comfortable with Jesus becoming a greater part of your life, and many of you will be in this state of mind, then that is because you are still satisfied with what you can do to make yourself satisfied with life. This is a commonplace human predicament. Jesus has the cure for this condition. Jesus does not see this evil in us and say; *well forget you, then.* No, He is faithful to resolve/judge this evil in we who are

His followers if we will humble ourselves by following Jesus into facing this difficulty in our relationship with God.

I am one of those metaphorical younger brothers, considered the losers in human society, that God selects to show off His ability. This has made it somewhat easier for me to see that I need God's strength. Even so, I too have places in my life where I feel I am doing pretty well without God's help. I don't like facing this in me, but it is there. And facing it is how I come to get freed from it by God. I recommend this course of action to you as well.

Revelation 3:21 He that overcometh, I will give to him to sit down with me in my throne, as I also overcame, and sat down with my Father in his throne.

Jesus says, If you conquer your self-righteous, hypocritical, non-committal attitude, and come to commit to wholly trusting God to transform your wretched humanity, I will see to it that you have God's power and authority flowing through you (to sit with Me on My throne).

Revelation 3:22 He that hath an ear, let him hear what the Spirit saith to the churches.

If you want to hear what God has to say to you, then listen to what His Spirit is saying to the ecclesia. God is saying to us what Jesus just said to these seven churches, to Jesus' followers. If you want to hear from God, then hear what He is saying to each of these seven churches.

ON IDOLATRY

From The Schaff Herzog Encyclopedia of Religious Knowledge

Ahab and His Toleration of Jezebel's Idolatry

Ahab's reign is of great importance in the religious development of Israel and is marked by a bitter contest between the throne and the prophets. That Ahab had no intention of apostatizing from Yahweh, the god of his people, is shown by the names he gave his children; but to rule righteously, according to the conception of the prophets, did not suit his policy.

He tolerated the calf worship instituted by Jeroboam (I Kings *Iii.* 26 33), and, influenced by his Phoenician wife, introduced into Samaria the worship of the Syrian Baal (Melkarth), for whom he built in his capital a great temple with all the necessary paraphernalia. No doubt certain circles in Israel were shocked by this heathen worship, but the great majority saw in it no inconsistency with the Mosaic religion. It fell to Elijah to rebuke the people for "halting between two opinions"; but his voice, like that of other prophets who protested, had little effect. Jezebel tried to silence them by bloody persecutions, and Elijah complained that he was the only prophet of Yahweh left. It must not be imagined, however, that all so-called prophets of Yahweh had been killed; for Ahab, who still regarded himself as a worshiper of Yahweh, would hardly have permitted such an act. Those who did not oppose the worship of Baal were doubtless left alone, but in the eyes of Elijah, they were not much better than the prophets of Baal. After the event on Mount Carmel (I Kings xviii.) Jezebel saw the futility of trying to suppress the opposition to the worship of Baal, and the prophets who had kept in hiding could come and go freely.

Ahab and his wife were also denounced by Elijah for the crime committed against Naboth and his family, which led to signs of contrition on the king's part and a postponement to his son's days of the threatened retribution (I Kings xxi.; cf. II Kings ix. 21-26). Ahab's character and achievements are differently estimated. He was undoubtedly an able man, and desired to promote the welfare of his people; he was a brave warrior and died manfully. But in the estimation of many these virtues are outweighed by his weakness toward Jezebel, his short-sighted optimism after the victory at Aphek, and his lack of deep religious conviction and earnestness. (W. LuTz.)

I think that it is important to see that we, like Ahab, have unconscious intentions, which manifest as our toleration of Jezebel. We cannot serve YHWH and Ba'al both. And we cannot serve YHWH and Jezebel both. The fact that Ahab named his children with Yahwehistic names, only serves to show us how we can think we are following God, because of some genuine expressions of allegiance to God, and yet remain largely in the service of Satan/Baal. And God will not be fooled, as we so easily are.

We can call ourselves a Christian, and say we believe in Jesus, but if we decide to play it safe and form an alliance with self-righteous-legalism (Jezebel), God will judge this in us. And it is always, and only, our need to hedge our bets, to play it safe by allying with both parties in this conflict, which leads us to embrace legalism (which has always been by far the most popular religious approach among humans).

You may go to (johnbrusseau.com) to find more writings and some music by John Brusseau.